Contents

Introduction
How to use this book

'Macbeth' is one of Shakespeare's most famous plays. It is packed with drama, witchcraft and violence and has entertained millions of audiences for over four hundred years. Its universal appeal is obvious but tackling such a wide-ranging play in a short exam is a real challenge.

This guide is written and laid out to help you with your revision of 'Macbeth' and to ensure that your examination response is focused and clear. It is designed to show you how to address the most important elements that the examiner is looking for:

- language analysis
- **effective use of quotations**
- **exploration of themes**
- **understanding of character**
- **how a Jacobean audience would react to the play**

The book is divided into sections of characters and themes with a box at the top of each section which gives a strong, clear overview of the character or theme.

The section is then dealt with using 5-8 key quotations which are in **bold** font. Literary devices are in ***bold italics***.

The analysis of each quotation relates directly to the theme or character. Some of the points are fairly straightforward and some are much more analytical.

The context is added at the end to show how it can be woven into an answer with a relevant quotation. Context means the social, historical and literary influences of the time that Shakespeare was writing in and how these are reflected in the play.

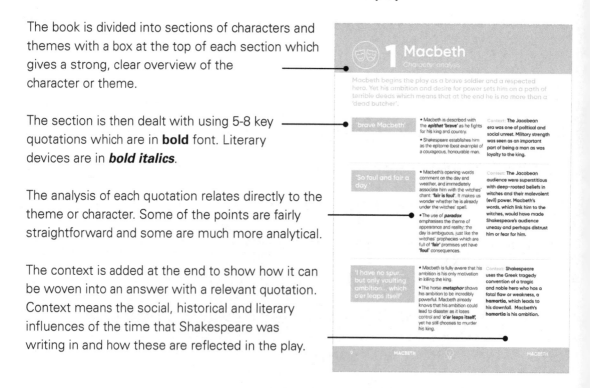

There is also a yellow box entitled 'Grade 9 Exploration' in each chapter. This shows you how you can look at alternative interpretations of the play, which are crucial for gaining a grade of 7 or above.

Look out for the colourful mindmap. It condenses four main points from the chapter, including the Grade 9 Exploration box, into four strands.

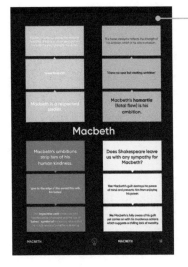

The information is in a shortened format; if you want to keep your revision really focused, use the mind map to make sure you remember the key features of the chapter.

Next comes a sample essay question. This is based on an extract from the play and the question is underneath. Depending on which exam board you are using, the wording will be different but that's fine; the essay question and plan will still be incredibly useful.

The sample essay answer follows. This is based on a 4-5 paragraph formula which answers the question clearly and analytically. The font is small as there is so much detail but, if you are wondering what a top level answer looks like, do read it carefully.

In each chapter, there is a box with essential exam tips: lots of good ideas and reminders that will help you on exam day.

At the back of the book, you will find a handy glossary of all the literary terms with examples and there's a list of the quotations, complete with act and scene references.

Timeline
Plot Summary

'Macbeth' is a story which covers huge political upheaval in Scotland but also documents the personal tale of a man whose ambition leads to his downfall. The action of the play spans over several months and moves from Scotland's battlefields to Macbeth's castle to the English court and back to Scotland. It isn't necessary to know exactly what happens in each scene; the timeline below outlines the main events over the course of the play.

Act 1

- The story starts with a bloody civil war. King Duncan rewards Macbeth for his loyalty in battle with the title of Thane of Cawdor.

- The witches meet Macbeth and make their predictions that Macbeth will be Thane of Cawdor and then King.

- They also predict that Banquo's children will be kings.

- Macbeth is told that he has been named the new Thane of Cawdor by King Duncan.

- He immediately starts to wonder if the prophecy about him becoming king will come true and whether he should make sure that it does happen by murdering King Duncan.

- Lady Macbeth and Macbeth begin to plan their murder of King Duncan.

- Duncan arrives at the Macbeths' castle.

- The Macbeths' plan is finalised as they plot to kill Duncan and blame it on the servants.

Act 2

- Macbeth kills Duncan.

- In the confusion afterwards, Malcolm (Duncan's eldest son) flees to England.

- Macbeth is crowned king but he does not have the loyalty of all the Scottish noblemen.

Act 3

- Macbeth is king but he is not confident in his new position. He is worried that the witches' prophecy about Banquo's children becoming kings so he hires murderers to kill Banquo and his son, Fleance.

- The murderers kill Banquo but Fleance escapes.

- Banquo's ghost comes to the feast that Macbeth is holding, sending Macbeth into a state of fear and confusion.

- Macduff, a Scottish thane, is planning to organise an army to attack Macbeth and replace him with Malcolm.

Act 4

- Macbeth visits the witches. They show him visions which tell him three things;

    1. To be careful of Macduff.

    2. That no man born of woman can kill Macbeth.

    3. That he will never be defeated until Birnam Wood moves to Dunsinane Hill.

- Macbeth believes the witches.

- Macbeth sends his soldiers to kill Macduff's wife and children.

- Macduff hears the news of his family's murder and vows to have his revenge on Macbeth.

- He allies himself with Malcolm who now has a large army.

Act 5

- Lady Macbeth has gone mad, sleepwalking and washing her hands of imaginary blood.

- Malcom's army arrives in Scotland. The plan is for the soldiers cut down branches from Birnham Wood as a disguise.

- Macbeth feels safe because of the witches' predictions. He is told of Lady Macbeth's suicide.

- Macbeth and Macduff meet in battle.

- Macduff reveals that he was not born of woman as his mother had a Caesarean birth. They fight and Macbeth is killed.

- At the end, Malcolm becomes king of Scotland.

1 Macbeth
Character analysis

Macbeth begins the play as a brave soldier and a respected hero. Yet his ambition and desire for power sets him on a path of terrible deeds which means that at the end he is no more than a **'dead butcher'**.

'brave Macbeth' 	• Macbeth is described with the **epithet 'brave'** as he fights for his king and country. • Shakespeare establishes him as the epitome (best example) of a courageous, honourable man.	**Context:** The Jacobean era was one of political and social unrest. Military strength was seen as an important part of being a man as was loyalty to the king.
'so foul and fair a day '	• Macbeth's opening words comment on the day and weather, and immediately associate him with the witches' chant: **'fair is foul'**. It makes us wonder whether he is already under the witches' spell. • The use of **paradox** emphasises the theme of appearance and reality; the day is ambiguous, just like the witches' prophecies which are full of **'fair'** promises yet have **'foul'** consequences.	**Context:** The Jacobean audience were superstitious with deep-rooted beliefs in witches and their malevolent (evil) power. Macbeth's words, which link him to the witches, would have made Shakespeare's audience uneasy and perhaps distrust him or fear for him.
'I have no spur... but only vaulting ambition... which o'er leaps itself'	• Macbeth is fully aware that his ambition is his only motivation in killing the king. • The horse **metaphor** shows his ambition to be incredibly powerful. Macbeth already knows that his ambition could lead to disaster as it loses control and **'o'er leaps itself'**, yet he still chooses to murder his king.	**Context:** Shakespeare uses the Greek tragedy convention of a tragic and noble hero who has a fatal flaw or weakness, a **hamartia**, which leads to his downfall. Macbeth's **hamartia** is his ambition.

'when you durst do it, then you were a man'	• Macbeth is manipulated by Lady Macbeth, who uses ideas of manhood to control him. • She taunts him with a lack of courage, saying that a real man would kill the king.	
'I could not say 'Amen' 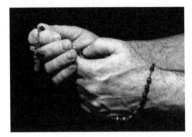	• Immediately after the regicide, Macbeth is consumed with guilt and is unable to say the traditional response to a religious blessing. His actions have placed him beyond God's love and comfort.	**Context:** Regicide (killing of a king/queen) was seen as an appalling crime because it was a crime against God. The Jacobeans believed in the divine right of kings, that God anointed (chose) the monarch. The audience would understand the sacrilegious nature of Macbeth's crime and appreciate his overwhelming guilt.
'my mind is full of scorpions'	• Macbeth finds that becoming king does not bring him happiness. • The **metaphor** shows that he is deeply troubled. The sense of pain and viciousness in this **image** allows the audience to understand his torment. We are not sure whether his mind is tortured with the guilt of regicide or the fear and suspicion that plagues him now that he is king.	
'give to the edge o' the sword/his wife, his babes' 	• Macbeth's desire for complete power leads him to commit despicable acts such as the murder of Macduff's family. • The **imperative verb** captures his cold-hearted sense of purpose and the use of **'babes'**, a **symbol** of innocence, illustrates that Macbeth is fully aware of what he is ordering. Ambition has stripped Macbeth of all compassion; he is now more monster than man. • Macduff's later grief acts as a **foil** to Macbeth's lack of emotion.	

'life's but a walking shadow, a poor player'	• Macbeth's last **soliloquy** reveals his thoughts after he hears the news of Lady Macbeth's death.
	• The **tone** is depressed and resigned as he reflects on the meaning of life. The **metaphor** suggests that life is without purpose, as devoid of substance as a shadow.
	• The **plosive** sounds of **'poor player'** reveal his bitterness as Macbeth realises that he has lost; his ambition has come to nothing. His words remind the audience that we are watching a play; a play that teaches us about the folly of mankind and the dangers of ambition.

Grade 9 Exploration:
Look at the character in a different way

Does Shakespeare leave us with any sympathy for Macbeth?

Yes: The pain of his last **soliloquy** shows his realisation that his actions have had no meaning and his lack of happiness in his kingship. The poetic control presents to us a man of sensitivity and intelligence, not the brutish **'dead butcher'** that Malcolm dismisses him as. Furthermore, there is a sense of nobility at the end when he dies with honour and bravery as he rises to the challenge of fighting Macduff, stating **'bear-like, I must stay the course'**. The **simile** of **'bear-like'** reflects his determination to die bravely. Bears were seen as noble and the comparison shows that, despite his crimes, Macbeth still retains the vestiges of nobility. At the end, he is still **'brave Macbeth'** and the epitome of a fearless fighter.

No: His actions mark him as a man of brutal violence. The regicide places him beyond redemption for a Jacobean audience, and all audiences would be horrified by his calculated **'slaughter'** in Act 4 of Macduff's wife and children.

Shakespeare used the structure of Greek tragedy to create a hero who has a hamartia (fatal flaw). In Macbeth's case, this **hamartia** is ambition which changes him from an honourable man to a violent murderer. Yet we still see human qualities and this makes us question ourselves as to how far we would go for power and feel pathos (pity) at how far Macbeth has fallen.

Essential Exam Tips

☑ Make at least three points based on the extract.

☑ When writing about the play as a whole, refer to at least three other parts of the text.

Macbeth begins the play as the epitome (example) of a strong, courageous soldier. He ends the play fighting to the death.

The horse *metaphor* reflects the strength of his ambition which is his only motivation.

'brave Macbeth'

'I have no spur but vaulting ambition'

Macbeth is a respected soldier.

Macbeth's *hamartia* (fatal flaw) is his ambition.

Macbeth

Macbeth's ambitions strip him of his human kindness.

Does Shakespeare leave us with any sympathy for Macbeth?

'give to the edge o' the sword/his wife, his babes'

Yes: Macbeth's guilt destroys his peace of mind and prevents him from enjoying his power.

The *imperative verb* captures his cold-hearted sense of purpose and the use of **'babes'**, *symbol of* innocence, shows that he is fully aware of what he is ordering.

No: Macbeth is fully aware of his guilt yet carries on with his murderous actions which suggests a chilling lack of morality.

Read the following extract from Act 5 Scene 5 of 'Macbeth'.
Answer both questions below the text.

At this point in the play, Macbeth has just received news of Lady Macbeth's death.

MACBETH:
She should have died hereafter;
There would have been a time for such a word.
To-morrow, and to-morrow, and to-morrow,
Creeps in this petty pace from day to day
To the last syllable of recorded time,
And all our yesterdays have lighted fools
The way to dusty death. Out, out, brief candle!
Life's but a walking shadow, a poor player
That struts and frets his hour upon the stage
And then is heard no more: it is a tale
Told by an idiot, full of sound and fury,
Signifying nothing.
Enter a Messenger
Thou comest to use thy tongue; thy story quickly.

a) Discuss how the character of Macbeth is presented in this extract.

b) Discuss how the character of Macbeth is presented in the play as a whole.

☑ Start with an overview

Macbeth, the eponymous hero, is presented in this extract as a man who is compelled to contemplate just how much meaning his life has. His despair at the emptiness of his future life is a sharp contrast with his earlier fantasy of the exciting, powerful life of a king that he so desired. Throughout the play, the audience witnesses the changes in Macbeth's character as he pays the price for fulfilling his **'black and deep desires'**.

☑ Make the point that Macbeth is presented as a man who is defeated

In the extract, there is ambiguity in Macbeth's response to his wife's death as he says that **'she should have died hereafter'**. Where once she was his **'dearest partner in greatness'**, here he dismisses her death in one sentence. This could perhaps show his callousness (lack of emotion) which suggests his brutal killing sprees have stripped him of human qualities and he is now more monster than man. However, it could suggest a pain at her death; certainly he looks ahead at his future without her as empty and tedious. The **repetition** in his lines **'to-morrow, and to-morrow, and to-morrow'** shows a dreary weariness and the time **metaphor** reflects the monotony of his last time on earth. The **verb 'creeps'** captures how slowly the time passes as he contemplates a future without his wife and, with a conscience so disturbed it leaves him with a **'mind full of scorpions'**, he finally realises there will be no joy in his kingship. The **monosyllabic** phrase **'pace from day to day'** helps create this sense of monotony and the words **'recorded syllable'** presents time as something to be measured and counted out, not enjoyed. Here, we see Macbeth paying the price of his crime of killing Duncan and the Jacobean audience would have understood this, viewing the act of regicide as an appalling one because it was a sin against God. They believed that God anointed the monarch, who therefore ruled by divine right, and so killing this anointed king was a sacrilegious act. Macbeth's lack of happiness in his own kingship is a clear lesson to the contemporary audience: that committing treason and murder does not bring happiness or contentment.

☑ Move to the point that Macbeth confronts his own failure

Indeed, this lack of happiness dominates Macbeth's *soliloquy*. The *tone* in the line '**life's but a walking shadow, a poor player**' is depressed and resigned as Macbeth reflects on the meaning of life. The *metaphor* suggests that life is meaningless, as devoid (empty) of purpose or substance as a shadow. The *plosive* sounds of '**poor player**' reveal the bitterness as Macbeth realises that he has lost and his ambition has come to nothing. The theatre *metaphor* reminds the audience that we are watching a play, a play that teaches us about the folly of mankind and the dangers of ambition. Looking back at his life, Macbeth sees himself simply as an actor playing a part from a script, perhaps the script written for him by the witches. Certainly the deeply superstitious Jacobean audience would have believed in the power of the witches to determine the outcome of the play from the start. The *syntax* of the final line with the word **'nothing'** ending the *soliloquy* reinforces the sense of hopelessness and defeat that consumes Macbeth.

☑ Move on to the point that Macbeth has a public image and purpose

There is a sharp *contrast* between these private, despairing thoughts of Macbeth and the public, purposeful commander he is seen as when he addresses the messenger with **'thou comest to use thy tongue; thy story quickly.'** The abrupt imperious *tone* here which demands information marks him as a strong leader and one who acts with speed and authority. Jacobean audiences, living in an era of great political change and constant threat of war, valued strong leadership and certainly, in Act One, before we even meet him, Macbeth is highly praised for his part in winning the battle against the Norwegians and the traitor Cawdor. He is described with the *epithet* **'brave'** as he fights for his king and country and Shakespeare establishes him as the epitome of a brave, honourable man and one whose military skill is highly prized.

☑ Move on to discuss how Macbeth has changed since the start of the play

Yet Macbeth's ambition corrupts him as he begins to plot to kill King Duncan, admitting that **'I have no spur... but only vaulting ambition... which o'er leaps itself '**. He is fully aware that his ambition is his only motivation in killing the king and the horse *metaphor* shows his ambition to be incredibly powerful. Macbeth already knows that his ambition could lead to disaster as it loses control and **'o'er leaps itself'**, yet he still chooses to murder his king. Shakespeare uses the *structure* of Greek tragedy to create a hero who has a *hamartia*, a fatal flaw, and in Macbeth's case, this fatal flaw is ambition. Shakespeare was interested in ideas of free will and Macbeth does make deliberate choices throughout the play to fulfil his ambitions which leads him to his downfall. Yet it is also possible that Macbeth's ambition is controlled by the witches, intent on wreaking havoc on the world of humans. It is their prophecies that spark the fire of ambition within him and their power over him is evident in Macbeth's opening words in the play which comment on the day and weather as he says **'so foul and fair a day I have never seen'**. The audience immediately associates him with the witches' chant of **'fair is foul'** as it seems that even Macbeth's words are being manipulated by evil forces. The Jacobeans had deep-set beliefs in the existence of witches, and would have acknowledged their power in controlling Macbeth.

☑ Explore whether we feel any sympathy for him at the end

Macbeth's ambition leads him to commit terrible crimes which plunge Scotland into a bloody civil war. Malcolm leaves us with the damning *epithet* **'dead butcher'** and indeed it is perhaps hard to sympathise with the heartless killer that Macbeth has become. Macbeth's ruthless ambition has stripped him of all manly compassion; the slaughter of women and children reflects his lack of humanity while the regicide places him beyond redemption for a Jacobean audience. Yet the searing pain of his last *soliloquy* shows Macbeth's realisation that his actions have had no meaning; the poetic control presents to us a man of sensitivity and intelligence and we see his nobility again at the end as he courageously says **'bear-like, I must fight the course'**. The *simile* of **'bear-like'** captures his determination to die bravely as bears were seen as noble; the comparison shows that, despite his crimes, Macbeth still retains the vestiges of honour. He does not die a coward's death and, at the end, he is still **'brave Macbeth'** and the epitome of a fearless fighter. By the end of the play, the audience has witnessed how Macbeth's fatal ambition destroys him, and this makes us question ourselves as to how far we would go to fulfil our desires, and to feel pity at just how far Macbeth has fallen.

2 Lady Macbeth
Character analysis

Lady Macbeth is the driving force behind Macbeth's killing of King Duncan but her desire for power leaves her broken and desperate.

'dearest partner in greatness'

- Macbeth addresses Lady Macbeth in his letter.
- The **superlative 'dearest'** shows the love that he has for his wife. **'Partner'** implies an equal, loving relationship.
- The **noun 'greatness'** suggests the ambition that already lies in them both.

'Come, you spirits... unsex me here... come'

- Lady Macbeth turns to the forces of evil and welcomes the dark spirits who will strip her of her femininity and allow her to commit murder.
- The use of the **imperative verb 'come'** shows that she deliberately turns to the forces of evil and embraces their power.
- The **repetition** of **'come'** makes it sound as if she is casting a spell, and therefore her language links her with the witches.

Context: The Jacobean audience were highly superstitious and firmly believed in the power of the supernatural. Lady Macbeth's decision to turn to the evil spirits would have been deeply disturbing to contemporary audiences.

'Look like the innocent flower/ but be the serpent under't'

- Lady Macbeth urges Macbeth to deceive everyone as they plan the king's murder.
- The **enjambment** and the turning point of the word **'but'** highlight her deliberate slyness and the **contrast** between the outward appearance and the inner reality.
- The **imperative verb 'look'** highlights her power over her husband as she gives him commands.

Context: The imagery reminds the church-going Jacobean audience of the serpent in the Garden of Eden as Lady Macbeth's language links her to the weak woman who tempted Adam to disobey God. Shakespeare shows her as manipulative and sinful, deliberately playing on contemporary perceptions of women.

'pluck'd my nipple... dash'd the brains'

• Lady Macbeth says that she would kill her nursing baby rather than act in the cowardly way Macbeth is. Ambition has stripped her of all feminine qualities.

• The viciousness of this **image** is a potent (powerful) one. The **verb 'pluck'd'** is **onomatopoeic** which emphasises the violence with which Lady Macbeth is speaking.

Context: The Jacobean audience believed that women were natural nurturers, meek and subservient. Lady Macbeth's vocabulary would have been very shocking to a Jacobean audience who would find this completely unnatural.

'Had he not resembled my father as he slept, I had done it. My husband?'

• As Lady Macbeth waits for news of Duncan's murder, she reflects that she was unable to kill him herself. She has not lost all traces of humanity.

• The sudden switch from her thoughts to seeing or hearing her husband captures her nervousness. The short **interrogative sentence 'my husband?'** reflects this.

'Be innocent of the knowledge, dearest chuck'

• After becoming king, Macbeth begins to confide less and less in his wife, planning the murders of Banquo and Fleance on his own.

• Lady Macbeth's power over her husband fades as the play progresses. She is now not a **'partner'** but is a **'chuck'**. This perhaps shows that he no longer values her as highly as he did.

> **'All the perfumes of Arabia will not sweeten this little hand. O, O, O'**

- Lady Macbeth acknowledges in her madness the extent of her guilt as she tries to clean imaginary blood from her hands.

- The *image* of the heavy scents of the myriad (many types of) perfumes of an exotic land shows how nothing can eradicate her guilt.

- The *fragmented speech* of **'O, O, O'** reflects the lack of control she has over her mind; this is very different from Act 1 when she calls the spirits to her with such authority. In this scene, she uses *prose*, rather than the *blank verse* she used in earlier acts, showing again the descent into madness.

Grade 9 Exploration:
Look at the character in a different way

Does Shakespeare leave us with any sympathy for Lady Macbeth?

Yes: Her ambition brings her no happiness and the play documents the change in Lady Macbeth from a strong ambitious woman to a broken wreck. At the end, the serving woman who watches her anguished sleepwalking says **'I would not have such a heart in my bosom'**, which directs the audience's response to feel the pathos (pity) of the disintegration of her mind, her power and her relationship with her husband. We, too, would not have such a tortured conscience for all the world.

No: Malcolm's final summary of Lady Macbeth as a **'fiend-like queen'** defines her. She deliberately chooses a path of evil and there is justice in the ending of the play and her self-inflicted death.

Regicide (killing of a king or queen) was seen as an appalling act because it was a crime against God. The Jacobeans believed in the divine right of kings, that God anointed (chose) the monarch and Lady Macbeth's part in such a crime would have been viewed as unforgivable.

Essential Exam Tips

☑ Look for lines which show things you already know about the character e.g. you know that Lady Macbeth is ambitious so look for a line that shows this.

☑ Analyse at least two quotations in detail, using literary terminology (simile/ alliteration/ repetition etc).

Lady Macbeth

The use of the *imperative verb* 'come' shows that she deliberately turns to the forces of evil.
The *repetition* makes it sound as if she is casting a spell.

'Come, you spirits... come'

Lady Macbeth turns to the supernatural to reject her feminine side.

The *enjambment* and the turning point of the word **'but'** highlight the deliberate slyness and the contrast between the outward appearance and the inner reality.

'Look like the innocent flower/But be the serpent under't'

Lady Macbeth manipulates her husband and the Scottish lords.

Lady Macbeth's mind disintegrates with guilt.

'All the perfumes of Arabia will not sweeten this little hand. O, O, O'

The *image* shows how nothing can take away her guilt. The *fragmented* 'O O O' reflects how she has lost control of her mind.

Does the audience have any sympathy for her?

Yes: Her guilt destroys her peace of mind and prevents her from enjoying her power.

No: Lady Macbeth deliberately chooses a path of evil which suggests a chilling lack of morality.

Sample GCSE Exam Question

Read the following extract from Act 5 Scene 1 of 'Macbeth'.
Answer both questions below the text.

At this point in the play, Lady Macbeth is sleepwalking, watched by a doctor and a servant.

LADY MACBETH:
Yet here's a spot.
DOCTOR:
Hark! she speaks: I will set down what comes from
her, to satisfy my remembrance the more strongly.
LADY MACBETH:
Out, damned spot! out, I say!–One: two: why,
then, 'tis time to do't.–Hell is murky!–Fie, my
lord, fie! a soldier, and afeard? What need we
fear who knows it, when none can call our power to account?–Yet who would have thought the old man to have
had so much blood in him.
DOCTOR:
Do you mark that?
LADY MACBETH:
The thane of Fife had a wife: where is she now?–
What, will these hands ne'er be clean?–No more o'
that, my lord, no more o' that: you mar all with
this starting.

a) Write about how Lady Macbeth is presented in this extract.
b) Write about how Lady Macbeth is presented in the play.

 # Sample GCSE Exam Answer

 Start with an overview

Lady Macbeth is the driving force behind Macbeth's killing of King Duncan but her desire for power leaves her broken and desperate. In this extract, the audience sees her trying to wash imaginary blood from her hands in a frenzy of guilt-induced madness; whether we sympathise with her anguished state or feel that she deserves her mental torment is open to interpretation.

 **Make the point that Lady Macbeth is clearly overcome with guilt**

In the extract, Lady Macbeth tries to wash her hands of imaginary blood, saying **'out, damned spot! Out!'** The *imperative verb* **'out'** is *repeated*, displaying a desperate desire to clear her conscience. The *repetition* shows her anxiety as there is no sense of control in her *imperative verbs* here; the *repetition* makes her sound frantic and panicked, not a woman of authority. We are sharply reminded of her dismissive **'a little water clears us of this deed'** in Act 2. It is ironic that she is the one who is now consumed with guilt when then she was impatient with Macbeth's scruples and also ironic that she, who was so deceptive in the earlier stages of the play, is now openly displaying her guilt. Her fear at her own guilt is seen in the words **'hell is murky!'** suggesting that she is aware of how her crimes have put her beyond redemption and she is destined for the darkness of hell. The Jacobean audience would have understood this guilt and the consequences of regicide, seeing the crime as an appalling one because it was a sin against God. They believed that God anointed the monarch, who therefore ruled by divine right, and so killing this anointed king was a sacrilegious act. Lady Macbeth's mental turmoil is a clear lesson to the contemporary audience: that committing treason and murdering the king does not bring happiness or contentment. Interestingly, in the **soliloquy** in Act 1, Lady Macbeth actively seeks out darkness yet by Act 5, she is desperate to be clean and fears the **'murky'** visions of hell that she can see. Shakespeare perhaps uses this progression of her character to highlight just how dangerous ambition can be.

✔ Develop the point about how the guilt is sending her mad

Lady Macbeth is a broken woman in Act 5 whose mind flits from one dreadful crime to another- **'the old man ... had so much blood in him… the Thane of Fife had a wife'**. The controlled **blank verse** that she used in Act 1 has collapsed into **fragmented prose**, reflecting her fall from the strong, ruthlessly ambitious woman to a guilt-racked sleepwalker whose mind struggles to form coherent sentences. The randomness of the subject matter and the **dashes** highlight how her mind is being tormented by her crimes. The lines **'the old man... had so much blood in him'** remind us of the horror of the king's murder; the **noun phrase** **'old man'** emphasises how vulnerable Duncan was and the **phrase** **'so much blood in him'** how gory the crime was, and the audience is repelled by this. Yet we are also reminded of how she was innocent of Macduff's family's slaughter; the confused **question** **'where is she now?'**, referring to the Thane of Fife's wife, tells us that Macbeth acted alone for that crime and that Lady Macbeth arguably does not share in the blame for that massacre.

✔ Explore how Lady Macbeth has changed since the beginning of the play

The Lady Macbeth in the extract is very different to the purposeful woman in Act 1 who called the evil spirits to her with such control, commanding **'come, you spirits... come'**. Here, the use of the **imperative verb** shows that she has deliberately turned to the forces of evil and welcomes them in. The **repetition** of **'come'** makes it sound as if she is casting a spell, and therefore her language links her with the witches. This association was a a highly negative one for the Jacobean audience and for King James 1, who was deeply suspicious of the occult, to the extent that he wrote his own book 'Daemonologie' on the subject. Her sense of purpose in fulfilling her ambition is seen as she rejects her feminine side absolutely with her request to **'unsex me here'** and the heavy **monosyllabic** words emphasise the harsh determination of her actions. The controlled **rhythm** of the **soliloquy** mirrors her steady purpose as she allows her relentless ambition to overcome her morality.

✔ Explore how Lady Macbeth reflects, and also subverts, ideas of femininity

In Act 1, Lady Macbeth urges Macbeth to deceive everyone as they plan the king's murder, telling him to **'look like the innocent flower/ but be the serpent under't'**. The **enjambment** and the turning point of the word **'but'** highlight the deliberate slyness and the **contrast** between outward appearance and the inner reality. The **imagery** reminds the church-going Jacobean audience of the serpent in the Garden of Eden as Lady Macbeth's language links her to the weak woman who tempted Adam to disobey God. Shakespeare shows her as manipulative and sinful, deliberately playing on contemporary perceptions of women. Yet there is nothing sterotypical about her words that work to manipulate Macbeth; Lady Macbeth says that she would kill her nursing baby and **'pluck'd the nipple... dash'd the brains'** rather than act in the cowardly way Macbeth is. Ambition has stripped her of all feminine qualities. The viciousness of this **image** is a potent one. The **verb 'pluck'd'** is **onomatopoeic** which emphasises the violence with which Lady Macbeth is speaking. The Jacobean audience believed that women were natural nurturers, meek and subservient; her **vocabulary** would have been very shocking and unnatural.

✔ Explore whether we feel any sympathy for Lady Macbeth

It is interesting to consider how sympathetic a character she is and directors can present her in different ways. Her ambition brings her no happiness and the play documents the change in Lady Macbeth from strong ambitious woman to a broken wreck. At the end, the serving woman who watches her anguished sleepwalk says **'I would not have such a heart in my bosom'** which directs the audience's response to feel the pathos (pity) of the disintegration of Lady Macbeth's mind, her power and her relationship with her husband. We, too, would not have such a tortured conscience for all the world. Whether we despise Lady Macbeth, agreeing with Malcolm's definition that she is a **'fiend-like'** queen and feeling that she is deservedly punished at the end, or whether we sympathise with her evident torture, it is clear that the consequences of ambition carry a very high price indeed and that we should consider carefully before acting on our own **'black and deep desires'**.

King Duncan is murdered at the start of Act 2 yet his portrayal as a man and as a king is important in exploring the role of kingship in 'Macbeth.'

'Go pronounce his present death and with his former title greet Macbeth'

- Duncan instructs Ross (a lord) to have the Thane of Cawdor executed and to give the title to Macbeth as a reward for his loyalty.

- Shakespeare presents Duncan throughout this scene as a strong king; the **monosyllabic imperative verb 'go'** is used to show his authority.

- He makes decisions quickly and decisively; an important quality given the day of bloodshed and uncertainty.

Context: Strong rule was very important in the bloody, uncertain Tudor and Stuart times. Duncan's decisive actions in punishing a traitor would have been approved of by Shakespeare's audience.

'He was a gentleman on whom I built/An absolute trust'

- Duncan talks of how he completely trusted the traitor Cawdor.

- There is **dramatic irony** here as the **stage direction** immediately after these words has Macbeth entering. The audience knows that Macbeth is already considering murdering the king so **tension** is created when Duncan then calls Macbeth **'worthiest cousin'**.

- The **superlative 'worthiest'** reflects just how **'absolute'** is the trust he holds for Macbeth, and only the audience knows how wrong Duncan is to do so.

'I have begun to plant thee'

- Duncan tells Macbeth how he will nurture and support him.

- The positive **metaphor** of gardening establishes Duncan as someone who allows his kingdom to naturally grow and prosper.

- There is clear **contrast** between Duncan's leadership, which allows the country to grow, and Macbeth's later kingship, which destroys.

Context: The imagery of nature and growth links to the Bible, highlighting Duncan's status as God's anointed king to the religious Jacobean audience.

'so meek... that his virtues/will plead like angels, trumpet-tongued'

- As Macbeth wonders whether to kill Duncan, he thinks about how Duncan is such a good man and a great king.

- Duncan here is associated with celestial (heavenly) qualities. The **simile** shows Duncan to be so good that his virtues (good qualities) are angelic. The **alliteration** of **'trumpet-tongued'** reflects the blast of sound, like a heraldic trumpet, which suggests how loudly Duncan's qualities should be celebrated.

Context: **Shakespeare used an old source, Holinshed's Chronicles, as a basis for 'Macbeth'. In this original story, Duncan was an imperfect king; Shakespeare deliberately changed this in his version to create a saint-like king to flatter James 1 to whom the play was orginally performed.**

'most sacrilegious murder hath broke ope/The Lord's anointed temple, and stole thence the life o' the building!'

- Macduff expresses his complete horror at seeing Duncan's dead body by **personifying** murder as a thief.

- The religious **imagery** reflects the magnitude (strength) of the crime. Duncan is seen as an anointed temple, someone sacred and untouchable. The **plosive** sound of **'broke'** reflects the violence of the crime against someone so pure.

- There are many references to the disruption in nature that this murder has caused; Lennox states that the **'night has been unruly'** and **'the earth did shake'** which reflects how nature has been disturbed by the dreadful, sacrilegious crime of killing Duncan.

Context: **Regicide (killing of a king) was seen as an appalling crime because it was a sin against God. The Jacobeans believed in the divine right of kings, that God anointed (chose) the monarch. Murdering a king disrupted the natural order and would have been completely condemned by an audience for whom Guy Fawkes' Gunpowder Plot was a recent memory.**

• Malcolm's words conclude the play; this fitted in with the literary convention of the time. It is significant that the final words are given to the most senior figure, acknowledging his authority.

• This authority is further emphasised by the use of the **majestic plural pronoun 'we'** which includes the man, God, the Law and the State. Jacobean society believed in a rigid social structure with the monarch as central to society.

• They also believed in the Divine Right of Kings, and Malcolm's humble words **'by the grace of Grace'** refer to God's role and remind the audience that Malcolm, as direct heir to Duncan, rules by this Divine Right.

Grade 9 Exploration:
Look at the character in a different way

Is Duncan a perfect king?

Yes: He is decisive from the opening and his gracious, measured speech marks him as a noble, honourable king. The description of his dead body emphasises this perfection with his **'silver skin laced with his golden blood'**. The **metaphors** link him to highly valued metals which establish him as holy and precious.

No: He is reliant on violent men to fight his battles for him. Also, the play opens with the nation in a state of treachery and violence which suggests that Duncan is not a strong king and is too **'meek'**. Perhaps Shakespeare is reminding the Jacobean audience, who were living in turbulent times, that a strong leader is crucial to maintain order. Duncan also shows great error of judgement. He has already been deceived by one of his lords, the Thane of Cawdor, who has fought with the Norwegians against him, but he shows no better judgement when he trusts Macbeth. It is perhaps Malcolm, strong, gracious and cautious, who is the epitome of a perfect king.

 # Essential Exam Tips

☑ Try to embed quotations (see sample essay on the next page)

☑ Spend 5 minutes planning your answer; this helps you organise your ideas into a structure that is clear for the examiner.

The use of the *imperative verb* 'go' shows his authority. Jacobean audiences valued strong leadership.

The positive *metaphor* of gardening establishes Duncan as someone who allows his kingdom to naturally grow and prosper.

'Go pronounce his present death'

'I have begun to plant thee'

Duncan shows strong leadership as he decisively deals with the traitor Cawdor.

Duncan is a great king, showing care and love for his country.

King Duncan

Duncan's murder is a crime against God.

Is Duncan a perfect king?

'most sacrilegious murder hath broke ope... the Lord's anointed temple'

Yes: Duncan is so good **'his virtues/will plead like angels'**. He is associated with celestial *imagery*, showing his holy nature.

The religious *imagery* reflects the magnitude (strength) of the crime. Duncan is seen as an anointed temple- someone sacred and untouchable.

No: Duncan is too gullible, saying that Cawdor **'was a gentleman on whom I built/An absolute trust'**. Yet he does not learn his lesson and trusts Macbeth.

Read the following extract from Act 1 Scene 6 of 'Macbeth'.
Answer both questions below the text.

At this point in the play, King Duncan has just arrived to stay the night at the Macbeths' castle.

DUNCAN:
Where's the Thane of Cawdor?
We coursed him at the heels, and had a purpose
To be his purveyor: but he rides well;
And his great love, sharp as his spur, hath holp him
To his home before us. Fair and noble hostess,
We are your guest to-night.

LADY MACBETH:
Your servants ever
Have theirs, themselves and what is theirs, in compt,
To make their audit at your highness' pleasure,
Still to return your own.

DUNCAN:
Give me your hand;
Conduct me to mine host: we love him highly,
And shall continue our graces towards him.
By your leave, hostess.

a) Discuss how King Duncan and kingship are presented in this extract.

b) Discuss how King Duncan and kingship are presented in the play as a whole.

 Sample GCSE Exam Answer

☑ Start with an overview

King Duncan is murdered at the start of Act 2 yet his portrayal as a man and as a king is important in exploring the role of kingship in 'Macbeth'. In this extract, Duncan has just won the battle against the Norwegians and the traitor Cawdor; he visits the Macbeths' castle, unaware of the plot against his life. He is undoubtedly a polite, gracious guest but his success as a king is more open to interpretation.

☑ Make the point that Duncan is a king clearly in control

In the extract, Duncan is a king in control and his use of the ***imperative verbs*** '**give**' and '**conduct**' help to establish a sense of authority. This would have been expected by the Jacobean audience who believed in the Great Chain of Being, a rigid social structure in which everyone in society had his/her place with the king at the top. In this scene, Duncan's authority has just been cemented by his victory over the Norwegians; military strength was a skill highly prized in the turbulent times of the seventeenth century. This authority is also shown in his use of the ***majestic royal plural*** '**we**' which reflects how his authority comes from his position; he is not just a man, he represents the law, the State and God's authority and this is summed up by the use of '**we**' rather than 'I'.

☑ Explore how Lady Macbeth responds to him

Lady Macbeth shows great respect for Duncan's authority as her flowery language puts herself and Macbeth at **'your highness' pleasure'**. Under the social conventions of the time, she would have been expected to offer welcome to anyone of rank. Yet the theme of appearance and reality is evident here and there is ***dramatic irony*** as the audience clearly remembers the previous scene where Lady Macbeth has plotted with Macbeth to kill the king and doubts the sincerity of her words. Yet Duncan is clearly completely taken in by his deceitful hostess and indeed, elsewhere in the play, he is seen as a character who trusts too easily. Earlier in the act, Duncan talks of how he had complete confidence in the traitor Cawdor who 'was a gentleman on whom I built/An absolute trust', the intensifier 'absolute' reminding us of the extent of his faith. There is ***dramatic irony*** here as the ***stage direction*** immediately after these words has Macbeth entering. The audience knows that Macbeth is already considering murdering the king so ***tension*** is created when Duncan then calls Macbeth **'worthiest cousin'**. The ***superlative*** **'worthiest'** reflects just how **'absolute'** is the trust he holds for Macbeth, and only the audience knows how wrong Duncan is to do so. It seems that Duncan is a poor judge of character and that allows us to question how good a king he is.

☑ Make the point that Duncan is a gracious and pleasant character

Duncan shows excellent social skills with his interaction with Lady Macbeth. He makes a joke about **'coursing'** (chasing) Macbeth back to the castle, showing an easy humour. He is very gracious, addressing her with a pair of ***adjectives*** that compliment her- **'fair and noble'** -and is polite with his **'by your leave'**. He presents himself as a genuinely pleasant person and Macbeth acknowledges this later when he agonises over whether to kill him, saying Duncan is **'so meek...that his virtues/will plead like angels, trumpet-tongued'**. Duncan here is associated with celestial (heavenly) qualities as the ***simile*** shows Duncan to be so good, his virtues (good qualities) are angelic. The ***alliteration*** of **'trumpet tongued'** reflects the blast of sound, like a heraldic trumpet, which suggests how loudly Duncan's qualities should be celebrated. Shakespeare used an old source, Holinshed's Chronicles, as a basis for 'Macbeth'. In the original story, Duncan was an imperfect king; Shakespeare deliberately changes this in his version to create a saint-like king to flatter James 1 to whom the play was first performed. Duncan's perfection also acts as a ***foil*** to Macbeth's later brutal kingship, reminding the audience of how a true and noble king should behave.

☑ Move on to show how killing Duncan is seen as a horrific act

Macduff expresses his complete horror at seeing Duncan's dead body by ***personifying*** murder as a thief: **'most sacrilegious murder hath broke ope/The Lord's anointed temple, and stole thence the life o' the building!'** The religious ***imagery*** reflects the magnitude (strength) of the crime. Duncan is seen as an anointed temple, someone sacred and untouchable, and the ***plosive*** sound of **'broke'** shows the horrific violence of the crime against someone so pure. Regicide was seen as an appalling crime because it was a sin against God. The Jacobeans believed in the divine right of kings, that God anointed (chose) the monarch. This was part of the belief in the Great Chain of Being, that everyone in society had his/her place with the king at the top. Murdering a king disrupted the natural order and would have been condemned by an audience for whom Guy Fawkes' Gunpowder Plot was a very recent memory. Shakespeare's 'Macbeth' reminds the audience of the sanctity of kingship.

☑ Explore whether Duncan is a perfect king

Arguably, Shakespeare presents Duncan as a perfect king. He is decisive from the opening as he orders the death of Cawdor, and his gracious, measured speech marks him as a noble, honourable king. The description of his dead body emphasises this perfection with his **'silver skin laced with his golden blood'**. The ***metaphors*** link to him highly valued metals which show him as holy and precious. However, he is reliant on violent men to fight his battles for him and indeed, the play opens with the nation in a state of treachery and violence which suggests that Duncan is not a strong king. Perhaps Shakespeare is reminding the Jacobean audience, who were living in turbulent times, that a strong leader is crucial to maintain order. Duncan also shows great error of judgement in trusting too quickly. It is perhaps his son Malcolm, strong, gracious and cautious, who is the epitome of a perfect king and whose succession reassures the audience that peace will return to Scotland.

4 Malcolm
Character analysis

Malcolm flees to England after the murder of his father, King Duncan, yet returns with an army to defeat Macbeth and claim his throne. His portrayal as a man and a king is important in exploring the role of kingship in 'Macbeth.'

'This murderous shaft that's shot/ Hath not yet lighted'

- When his father Duncan is murdered, Malcolm takes immediate actions to avoid being the next to be killed; he slips away to England before the **'shaft'** can **'light'** on him.

- This **metaphor** of an arrow shows that Malcolm is fully aware of the danger he is in.

- Malcolm's actions can be interpreted in different ways by audiences; are his actions wise or cowardly?

- Malcolm's decision to flee drives the plot as he leaves the way clear for Macbeth to take the crown. This adds to the drama as the audience knows that Scotland is in the hands of a proven murderer and will be anxious about what Macbeth will do next.

'reconciled my thoughts/To thy good truth and honour'

- When Macduff comes to join Malcolm in England, Malcolm tests Macduff's loyalty by pretending to be evil. Macduff passes the test and Malcolm's mind is now reassured as to Macduff's honourable intentions.

- Malcolm shows himself as more cautious than his father, Duncan, who was too quick to put his **'absolute trust'** in others.

Context: The Jacobean audience lived in a world where betrayal and vying for power was common. They would approve of a king who proved to be shrewd.

'Dispute it like a man'

- Malcolm tells Macduff to revenge himself on Macbeth.

- Malcolm is seen as a strong man here. He refers to the idea of manhood being about honour and revenge.

- The audience is reassured by the way Malcolm is being presented. His strength of character and notions of honour suggest that he will make an effective leader of Scotland, in direct **contrast** to Macbeth's rule of bloodshed.

'Let every soldier hew him down a branch'

- Malcolm tells the soldiers to camouflage themselves with the trees from Birnam Wood.

- There is a sense of authority in the **imperative verb 'let'** and also a clear display of military acumen (skill) in his original idea about disguising his army.

- Malcolm is fully involved in the strategy of the battle. He seems different to his father, King Duncan, who kept a distance from battle. This gives the audience hope that Malcolm will prove a better leader.

Context: In Jacobean times, kings were expected to be able to lead armies at time of war. Shakespeare was writing at a time of great political and social change which often led to military conflict; Malcolm's military acumen (skill) would have been approved of.

'By the grace of Grace/We will perform in measure, time and place'

- Malcolm's words conclude the play; this fitted in with the literary convention of the time. It is significant that the final words are given to the most senior figure, acknowledging his authority.

- This authority is further emphasised by the use of the **majestic plural pronoun 'we'**, which includes the man, God, the Law and the State. Jacobean society believed in a rigid social structure with the monarch as central to society.

- They also believed in the divine right of kings, and Malcolm's humble words **'by the grace of Grace'** refer to God's role and remind the audience that Malcolm, as direct heir to Duncan, rules by this Divine Right.

Context: Shakespeare uses the classic five act play **structure** of the ancient Greeks which always ended with **resolution**. There is a sense of closure at the end of the play and the audience is reassured that lessons will be learned from the tragic deaths. The **rhyming couplets** in this final speech help give the play this sense of **resolution** and conclusion.

Grade 9 Exploration:
Look at the character in a different way

Is Malcolm just a *symbol* of authority?

Yes: Malcolm's primary role in the play is that of the rightful heir to the throne and we have little sense of him as a real character. He is simply used by Shakespeare to illustrate one of the main themes in the play, that of the nature of kingship, representing the natural order of society which is restored at the end of the play. He is a *symbol*, like his father; they both use *images* of nature and growth which are linked to the Bible such as talking of plans **'which would be planted newly'** to show how he will heal his homeland. This reminds us of his father, who tells Macbeth how he will nurture and support him, saying **'I have begun to plant thee'**. The positive *metaphors* of gardening reflect how Duncan and Malcolm are seen as men who allow their kingdom to naturally grow and prosper. The *imagery* of nature and growth links to the Bible, highlighting the status of both Duncan and Malcolm as God's anointed kings to the religious Jacobean audience. Malcolm, as Duncan's son, is just a figurehead of righteous rule.

No: Shakespeare creates a character who is cautious and compassionate. In Act 4, his testing of Macduff by pretending to be evil shows that he is clever and shrewd while he also displays a sensitive and compassionate side. When Macduff receives the terrible news of the slaughter of his family, Malcolm says **'give sorrow words'**, urging Macduff to express his grief. His humanity *contrasts* with the inhumanity of the murders and his kindness here highlights Macbeth's brutality. Malcolm is also a man of integrity and courage who can lead armies; he is far more than just a figurehead.

Essential Exam Tips

- ☑ Look at punctuation marks in the extract. Question marks indicate questions which suggest uncertainty and confusion. Exclamation marks suggest passion or violence or humour.

- ☑ Start revising for the exams early. Revising in ten minute bursts from the end of Year 10 can make a huge difference and reduces the last minute panic before your exams.

Malcolm is more cautious than his father, Duncan, who was too quick to put his **'absolute trust'** in others; Malcolm will make a better king.

There is a sense of authority in the *imperative verb*. Jacobean audiences, who lived in turbulent times, valued strong leadership.

▲

'reconciled my thoughts/To thy good truth and honour'

'Let every soldier hew him down a branch'

▲

Malcolm shows a cautious nature when he tests Macduff's loyalty.

Malcolm shows military skill and clear authority.

Malcolm

Malcolm ends the play as rightful heir and order is restored to Scotland.

Is Malcolm a 2D figurehead?

▼

'By the grace of Grace/We will perform in measure, time and place'

Yes: He is a *symbol* of the natural order of society which is restored at the end of the play and we have little sense of him as a man.

▼

Malcolm's humble words refer to God's role in kingship and remind the audience that Malcolm, as direct heir to Duncan, rules by divine right.

No: He is clever and cautious. His comforting of Macduff as he says **'give sorrow words'** reflects a gentle, compassionate side.

Sample GCSE Exam Question

Read the following extract from Act 5 Scene 8 of 'Macbeth'.
Answer both questions below the text.

At this point in the play, Malcolm is declared king of Scotland.

ALL:
Hail, King of Scotland!

FLOURISH

MALCOLM:
We shall not spend a large expense of time
Before we reckon with your several loves,
And make us even with you. My thanes and kinsmen,
Henceforth be earls, the first that ever Scotland
In such an honour named. What's more to do,
Which would be planted newly with the time,
As calling home our exiled friends abroad
That fled the snares of watchful tyranny;
Producing forth the cruel ministers
Of this dead butcher and his fiend-like queen,
Who, as 'tis thought, by self and violent hands
Took off her life; this, and what needful else
That calls upon us, by the grace of Grace,
We will perform in measure, time and place:
So, thanks to all at once and to each one,
Whom we invite to see us crown'd at Scone.

a) Write about how Malcolm and kingship are presented in this extract.

b) Write about how Malcolm and kingship are presented in the play as a whole.

Sample GCSE Exam Answer

 Make the point that Malcolm is seen as the rightful leader

In the extract, the characters unanimously acknowledge Malcolm as the figurehead of Scotland. The play started with violent rebellion but here there is a sense of unity as the order which was disrupted by the witches and Macbeth's terrible act is now restored through the ascension of the rightful leader- Malcolm. There is a sense of cohesion here which the Jacobean audience, who had only recently seen the union of Scotland and England, would appreciate. Shakespeare uses the classic five act play structure of the ancient Greeks which always ended with **resolution** and here there is a sense of closure with Malcolm cementing his power through inviting the noblemen **'to see us crown'd at Scone'**. The **rhyming couplets 'one/Scone'** conclude the play and help create an atmosphere of cohesion (unity).

☑ Move to the point that Malcolm and his kingship are firmly linked with religion

This cohesion is cemented with Malcolm's words which conclude the play; this fitted in with the literary

---

convention of the time. It is significant that the final words are given to the most senior figure, acknowledging his authority. This authority is further emphasised by the use of the **majestic plural pronoun 'we'** which includes the man, God, the Law and the state. Jacobean society believed in a rigid social structure with the monarch as central to society. They also believed in the divine right of kings, and Malcolm's humble words **'by the grace of Grace'** refer to God's role and remind the audience that Malcolm, as direct heir to Duncan, rules by this divine right. It would have been a reassuring end for Shakespeare's original audience.

☑ Move to the point that Malcolm and his leadership are seen as fair and positive

Malcolm promises to reward his loyal subjects by making his thanes **'earls'** and punishing those who supported Macbeth. Shakespeare uses a cyclical **structure** within the play; 'Macbeth' opened with a rebellion, reward and punishment and it concludes in the same way. Malcolm refers to the Macbeths as the **'dead butcher and his fiend-like queen'**. The derogatory **noun 'butcher'** shows us how kingship is not just about strength and reminds us that Macbeth has slaughtered innocents such as Macduff's wife and children in cold blood. Malcolm's brand of kingship is much more humane as he uses nature **metaphors** such as **'which would be planted newly'** to show how he will heal his homeland. This reminds us of his father, who tells Macbeth how he will nurture and support him, saying **'I have begun to plant thee'**. The positive **metaphor** of gardening shows how Duncan and Malcolm are seen as men who allow their kingdom to naturally grow and prosper. The **imagery** of nature and growth links to the Bible, highlighting the status of both Duncan and Malcolm as God's anointed kings to the religious Jacobean audience.

☑ Move on to show how Malcolm is seen as a strong, kind leader

Malcolm is seen as strong leader as he gives orders such as '**let every soldier hew him down a branch**', telling the soldiers to camouflage themselves with the trees from Birnam Woods. There is a sense of authority in the **imperative verb 'let'** and also a clear display of military acumen (skill) in his original idea about disguising his army. In Jacobean times, kings were expected to be able to lead armies at time of war. Shakespeare was writing at a time of great political and social change which often led to military conflict so Malcolm's military skill would have been approved of by contemporary audiences. However, he is not just a **symbol** of masculine strength; when news comes of the slaughter of Macduff's family, Malcolm urges Macduff to speak about his grief to prevent his heart from breaking, telling him to **'give sorrow words'**. Malcolm is seen as sensitive and compassionate with a real humanity here that encourages soldiers like Macduff to show their emotions. Malcolm's attitude **contrasts** with the inhumanity of Macbeth; he works as a **foil** to Macbeth to show how a real king and a real man should behave. There is clear **contrast** between Malcolm's leadership, which allows the country to grow, and Macbeth's kingship, which destroys.

☑ Explore whether Shakespeare has created a 'real' character or whether Malcolm is a figurehead

Malcolm's primary role in the play is that of the rightful heir to the throne. He is used by Shakespeare to illustrate one of the main themes in the play, that of the nature and the importance of kingship. He represents the natural order of society which is restored at the end of the play and we have little sense of him as a man rather than a figurehead. Yet this might not be a fair assessment; Shakespeare does create a character who is cautious and compassionate. In Act 4, when Macduff comes to join Malcolm in England, Malcolm tests Macduff's loyalty by pretending to be evil. Macduff passes the test and Malcolm's mind is now reassured as to Macduff's honourable intentions as he says he has **'reconciled my thoughts/To thy good truth and honour'**. Malcolm shows himself as more cautious than his father, Duncan, who was too quick to put his **'absolute trust'** in others. Later in that scene, Macduff receives the terrible news of the slaughter of his family and Malcolm comforts him saying **'give sorrow words'**. Malcolm displays a gentle, compassionate side. urging Macduff to express his grief. His humanity **contrasts** with the inhumanity of the murders and his kindness here highlights Macbeth's brutality. Malcolm is also a man of integrity and courage who can lead armies; he is more than just a figurehead. Ultimately, whether he is a complex character or more simply a **symbol** of good kingship, the contemporary audience and a modern one can only feel relief when Macbeth's brutal rule comes to an end and Malcolm ascends to the throne.

5 Banquo
Character analysis

In many ways, Banquo is similar to Macbeth; he is a warrior, a thane and a witness to the witches' predictions. The key difference comes in that Banquo does not succumb to evil. This costs him his life as he is murdered on Macbeth's orders.

'As sparrows eagles, or the hare the lion'

• Banquo is described by a soldier as incredibly brave in battle. He is no more frightened of the enemy than eagles would be of a sparrow. His portrayal is one of fearless warrior.

• The *image* compares him to noble, courageous beasts, signalling to the audience that Banquo is a man of honour and of valour.

Context: The Jacobean era was one of political and social unrest. Military strength was seen as an important part of being a man.

'Lesser than Macbeth, and greater' 'instruments of darkness'

• The witches' words are deliberately ambiguous (unclear) and confusing.

• Banquo recognises this sense of trickery in the mysterious words, later calling the witches **'instruments of darkness'** and warning how their predictions could lead to evil. This *metaphor*, which links the witches to a dark supernatural world, reflects his cautious nature.

Context: The witches were viewed by Christian Jacobean audiences as powerful, malicious figures, closely associated with the devil. Banquo's distrust of the witches would have been understood and approved of by the audience, just as Macbeth's words linking him to the witches make him a figure to be regarded with suspicion.

'I dreamt last night of the three weird sisters'

• Banquo's words reveal how he is still brooding on the predictions that his sons will be kings of Scotland. His open admission of how the witches have stayed on his mind is a direct **contrast** with Macbeth's lie of **'I think not of them'**. The theme of appearance and reality is shown here through Banquo's open, honest nature and Macbeth's deceit.

• Like Macbeth, he is clearly a man of ambition yet he does not act on this ambition. Shakespeare uses him as a *foil* (contrast) to Macbeth who does act on it.

'There if I grow, the harvest is your own'

- Banquo responds humbly to Duncan's love and praise, pledging his loyalty.

- He extends the nature **metaphor** that Duncan uses about how he will **'plant'** and **'grow'** his subjects. By developing the **metaphor**, we associate Banquo with nature, harmony and nurturing- all positive attributes.

- The nature **metaphor** also refers to images in the Bible, reminding the audience that God has chosen Duncan to rule over Scotland. Banquo's words show that he respects both his king and God.

- By picking up and using the king's words, he shows close links with Duncan which again aligns him to the side of good in the play.

'keep my... allegiance clear'

- Banquo firmly rejects Macbeth's subtle suggestion that Banquo should join Macbeth's side.

- Banquo is clear that he is loyal to King Duncan. His honourable nature is evident here.

Context: Holinshed's Chronicles was the source for Shakespeare when he wrote 'Macbeth'. Holinshed's Banquo was an accomplice in the murder of Duncan but Shakespeare changed this in his version so that Banquo is innocent. This was to flatter King James 1, who was monarch at the time Shakespeare wrote. James 1 claimed that Banquo was his ancestor, so Shakespeare was careful to present Banquo as loyal rather than the traitor that Holinshed portrayed.

'Enter the ghost of Banquo and sits in Macbeth's place'

- It is significant that Banquo takes Macbeth's seat, showing that, even though he is dead, Banquo is still a threat. His son, not Macbeth's, will indeed one day sit in that same throne.

- This is a dramatic and visual reminder to the audience of the witches' predictions and the relentless progress of fate; even though Macbeth has attempted to interfere with fate's plans for Banquo's heirs to inherit, fate cannot be stopped and Banquo's sons will still inherit from Macbeth.

'gory locks'	• Macbeth flinches from Banquo's ghost's hair which is soaked in blood.

• This *image* of ghastly violence emphasises to the audience how Banquo's murder was horrific and brutal.

• There is a powerful dramatic impact here as Banquo's ghost serves as a visual representation of Macbeth's guilt. Macbeth may have hired thugs to do his dirty work for him but he cannot escape the consequences of his violent decisions.

• For an audience, this is an incredibly tense scene.

Grade 9 Exploration:
Look at the character in a different way

Is Banquo a man of honour?

Yes: He is loyal to Duncan, firmly rejecting Macbeth's subtle advances to buy his loyalty; he tells Macbeth that he will **'keep my bosom franchised and allegiance clear'**. Jacobean notions of manhood was based on honour, and Banquo shows this honourable nature here. Shakespeare uses Banquo as a *foil* to Macbeth; both men are brave and ambitious yet Banquo does not allow his ambition to lead him into evil acts, unlike Macbeth.

No: He suspects Macbeth had **'play'dst most foully'** to win his throne. Yet he does nothing. Is this because he is a coward who is afraid of Macbeth? Or because he is ambitious and hopes to profit from the change in rule? Alternative views are that he is cunningly biding his time before exposing Macbeth or that he is a patriot who hopes that Scotland will prosper under Macbeth. Directors of productions are able to portray Banquo in a variety of ways; he is a complex character and not necessarily a hero.

Essential Exam Tips

☑ Leave time for checking through your work. One tip is to check each paragraph as you finish it before starting the next one.)

☑ When you read the extract, try to visualise the scene as you've seen it acted on stage or in a film. This will help you analyse ideas and characters.

The nature *metaphor* associates Banquo with harmony and nurturing, reflecting a character who is aligned with good, not evil.

Shakespeare changed Banquo's character from the source Holinshed's Chronicles to flatter King James.

'There if I grow, the harvest is your own'

'keep my... allegiance clear'

Banquo is a noble character, responding humbly to Duncan's love and praise.

Banquo is open and honest.

Banquo

Banquo is ambitious as he thinks of the witches' predictions.

Is Banquo really a man of honour?

'I dreamt last night of the three weird sisters'

Yes: He is loyal to Duncan, telling Macbeth that he will **'keep my... allegiance clear'**. He resists temptation and rejects evil.

Banquo hopes to be king, just like Macbeth. However, he does not act on his ambition and so provides a *foil* to Macbeth.

No: He suspects that Macbeth **'play'd most foully'** for the crown yet does nothing, perhaps because of his ambition.

Sample GCSE Exam Question

Read the following extract from Act 3 Scene 1 of 'Macbeth'. Answer both questions below the text.

At this point in the play, Macbeth is king of Scotland. Banquo is alone on stage.

BANQUO:
Thou hast it now: king, Cawdor, Glamis, all,
As the weird women promised, and, I fear,
Thou play'dst most foully for't: yet it was said
It should not stand in thy posterity,
But that myself should be the root and father
Of many kings. If there come truth from them–
As upon thee, Macbeth, their speeches shine–
Why, by the verities on thee made good,
May they not be my oracles as well,
And set me up in hope? But hush! no more.

a) How is Banquo presented in this extract?
b) How is Banquo presented in the play as a whole?

Sample GCSE Exam Answer

☑ Start with an overview

Shakespeare deliberately constructs the character of Banquo to act as a *foil* to Macbeth; both men are warriors, thanes and witnesses to the witches' predictions. Yet while Macbeth acts on his ambition and turns to evil, Banquo does not. At this point in the play, Banquo is becoming increasingly aware of just how compromised Macbeth is.

☑ Make the point that Banquo is uncertain about the future

Now Macbeth is king, Banquo is clearly brooding on how the witches' predictions have come true for Macbeth. This *soliloquy* allows the audience to see his inner thoughts which are a mixture of fear, anxiety and ambition. His *list* 'of Macbeth's titles **'king, Cawdor, Glamis, all'** shows how Macbeth has indeed risen to great power and the *syntax* of the *sentence structure* which places the **'all'** at the end of the *list* emphasises to the audience how absolute Macbeth's power is. There might well be a note of jealousy in this *list*, and this possible envy could also be see in his opening words **'thou hast it now'**. These *monosyllabic words* create a sense of someone pondering on the recent dramatic events; envy is one emotion but anxiety is another possible emotion. Certainly, there is a sense of fear as he suppresses his words at the end, saying **'hush! No more'**. Macbeth's Scotland is already one of tension and secrecy.

☑ Move to the point that Banquo is influenced by the witches

Banquo is superstitious and constantly thinks back to the **'weird women's'** prophecies. A belief in witches was common in Jacobean times; the Jacobean audience firmly believed in their existence and malevolent power. King James 1 was so convinced that he wrote his own book, Daemonologie, on the subject, and Banquo's superstition here would have been understood by contemporary audiences. It is interesting that his language shows a shift in attitude to the witches. When he first meets them, Banquo calls the witches **'instruments of darkness'** and warns how their predictions could lead to evil. This phrase, which links the witches to a dark, supernatural world, shows his cautious, careful nature. However, in Act 3 Sc 1, Banquo describes how the witches' **'speeches shine'**. Here, the *metaphor* suggests light, not darkness, through the *verb* **'shine'**, perhaps showing how Banquo too is now being seduced by his ambition and now sees their prophecies as positive.

☑ Move to the point that Banquo is a man of ambition

Banquo can see how Macbeth has benefited from his ambition and wonders whether he too can profit, asking if the witches can **'set me up in hope?'** His use of *interrogative sentence structure* shows that he is undecided and uncertain about whether his future will be as the witches suggested and whether he will be **'the root and father of many kings'**. Here we see the Jacobean's sense of the importance of progeny (bloodline descendants). As a thane in Scotland, Banquo is excited by the prospect of his descendants taking the throne; this would be an incredible honour and would result in an increase in his family's status and power..

☑ Move on to develop this point that Banquo acts as a foil to Macbeth

Shakespeare presents Banquo as a *foil* to Macbeth. Both are brave soldiers; at the start they are described by an officer as fearless in battle, no more intimidated of the enemy than **'eagles'** would be of a **'sparrow'.** The Jacobean era was one of political and social unrest, and military strength was seen as an important part of being a man, so before the audience meets them, they are given positive reports of the two men. Both men are also noble and ambitious yet there is a crucial difference: Macbeth acts on his ambition and kills the king but Banquo does not act on his ambition. He is a *symbol* of honourable manhood; he responds humbly to Duncan's love and praise, pledging his loyalty by declaring **'there if I grow, the harvest is your own'**. He extends the nature *metaphor* that Duncan uses about how he will **'plant'** and **'grow'** his subjects. This *metaphor* associates Banquo with nature and nurturing, both positive attributes and, by using the king's words, he shows close links with the King which again aligns him to the side of good in the play. Holinshed's Chronicles was the source that Shakespeare used when he wrote 'Macbeth' and in these Chronicles Banquo was an accomplice in the murder of Duncan. Shakespeare changed this so that Banquo is innocent. This was to flatter King James 1, who was monarch at the time Shakespeare wrote and who claimed that Banquo was his ancestor. So Shakespeare created a Banquo who is open, loyal and brave- everything a Jacobean audience would approve of. This open honesty is seen when Banquo tells Macbeth that **'I dreamt last night.. of the weird sisters'**, *contrasting* with Macbeth's lie **'I think not of them'**.

☑ Move onto the last point- that Banquo's character is open to interpretation

Banquo is traditionally seen as one of the heroes of 'Macbeth' whose terrible murder is one of the most dramatic moments in the play. Banquo's ghost returns to haunt Macbeth with the *stage direction* **'enter the ghost of Banquo and sits in Macbeth's place'**. It is significant that Banquo takes Macbeth's seat, showing that, even though he is dead, Banquo is still a threat. His son, not Macbeth's, will indeed one day sit in that same throne. This is a dramatic and visual reminder to the audience of the witches' predictions and the relentless progress of fate; even though Macbeth has attempted to interfere with fate's plans for Banquo's heirs to inherit, fate cannot be stopped and Banquo's sons will still inherit from Macbeth. There is hope for the audience that Scotland will once again be ruled by the children of Banquo, the epitome of a noble, honest man. However, this is one interpretation of Banquo's character and his personality might be more flawed than this. Banquo suspects Macbeth had **'play'dst most foully'** to win his throne. Yet he does nothing. Is this because he is a coward who is afraid of Macbeth? Or because he is ambitious and hopes to profit from the change in rule? Alternative views are that he is cunningly biding his time before exposing Macbeth or perhaps he is a patriot who hopes Scotland will prosper under Macbeth. Directors of productions are able to portray Banquo in a variety of ways; he is a complex character and not necessarily a hero.

The supernatural is at the heart of the play, influencing the characters and creating gripping dramatic tension.

'A desolate place: thunder and lightning. Enter three witches'

- The opening **setting** establishes an eerie atmosphere which immediately highlights the ominous (dangerous) presence of the witches and makes the audience uncomfortable.

- The thunder and lightning reflects a disturbance in nature. The **pathetic fallacy** warns the audience that a troubled time is coming.

- **Structurally**, Shakespeare opens the play with the **'three witches'**, emphasising their vital role.

Context: The Jacobean audience believed that disruption in nature (the macrocosm) reflected the human world (microcosm); Shakespeare uses the disturbance in nature to symbolise the potential disruption in the world of men. This would have created a sense of unease, compounded by the presence of the witches. The Jacobean audience firmly believed in their existence and malevolent (evil) power; King James 1 was so convinced that he wrote his own book, Daemonologie, on the subject. There is nothing comical or childish about these witches and Shakespeare's audience would have been chilled by their sinister presence.

'Fair is foul and foul is fair'

- The witches create a sense of confusion, showing us that things are not always as they seem.

- The use of **paradox** here highlights the power of the witches who will give Macbeth **'fair'** prophecies yet these will end up with **'foul'** consequences. The **repetition** of the **'f'** sounds emphasises a sense of forceful power and the **monosyllabic** words enhance the sense of the chanting of a spell.

- Shakespeare establishes an atmosphere of malevolent (evil) power right at the beginning, establishing a world where nothing is as it seems and is therefore dangerous. We remember this spell when we meet Macbeth who says **'so fair and foul a day'**, immediately linking him with the forces of evil.

'Thrice' (three)

- When the witches complete their spell before meeting Macbeth, **'thrice'** (three) is **repeated** to complete the spell of making the three prophecies (Glamis/Cawdor/King) that will convince Macbeth to kill the king.

- **'Three'** was a number associated with magic in Jacobean times so the audience would have known that magic was at work.

Context: Shakespeare is perhaps referencing the fates in Greek mythology, the three sisters who controlled the fate of men. This connection shows us how much power the witches have over Macbeth, influencing him so that he allows his ambition to overrule his better nature.

'Enter the ghost of Banquo and sits in Macbeth's place'

- Supernatural elements are also evident in the **'gory'** ghost of Banquo which adds enormous **dramatic tension**. It takes Macbeth's seat, showing that he is still a threat. Banquo's son, not Macbeth's, will indeed one day sit in that same throne.

- The ghost is a visual and dramatic reminder to the audience of how fate cannot be stopped.

- It is perhaps also a manifestation of Macbeth's guilty conscience.

'All this is so'

- The witches state that the apparitions they show him in Act 4 are true predictions, that their words speak the truth and that **'all this is so'**.

- The simple, **monosyllabic** statement of certainty shows utter conviction and **structurally**, the next scene is of the murder of Macduff's family to illustrate how quickly Macbeth acts on the witches' words, completely convinced in their accuracy.

- It is ironic that, by trying to eliminate Macduff as a threat, Macbeth ensures Macduff's anger and revenge that will end in Macbeth's death.

'Out, damned spot'

- As her mind disintegrates into madness, Lady Macbeth sees visions of blood.

- These visions could be sent by the evil spirits she once turned to in order to torment her and lead her to suicide.

- An alternative reading is that the visions could be hallucinations from a troubled mind.

Context: A superstitious Jacobean might well think the visions came from the supernatural while a modern audience would be more inclined to believe the psychological interpretation.

'juggling fiends'

- Macbeth condemns the witches when Macduff reveals that he was born via Caesarean birth.

- The *adjective* **'juggling'** shows that he finally understands that the witches have been playing with him.

Context: This is Macbeth's moment of *anagnorisis*, which comes from the tradition of Greek theatre and is the moment when a character makes a critical discovery. Here, Macbeth realises that his faith in the witches has been misplaced.

Grade 9 Exploration:
Look at the theme in a different way

Do the witches control the actions of the Macbeths?

Yes: The witches send the dagger in Act 2 to **'marshall'st'** (guide) Macbeth towards King Duncan's chamber. Macbeth might yet have decided against killing Duncan if the dagger had not guided him at this crucial time. The witches' spells manipulate throughout the play.

No: The dagger is simply a manifestation of Macbeth's own guilt. As the vision fades, he admits that **'there's no such thing'** and then with absolute purpose walks with his dagger to Duncan's chamber. He is control of his own actions and the witches are not responsible.

The Jacobeans believed in predetermination which is the philosophy that everything in life is mapped out for us by God or fate. However, Shakespeare was interested in the idea of self-determination, the way in which people control their own lives. This exploration is evident in the examination of the witches' role in the play; do they control the actions of the characters or do the characters have autonomy over their own decisions?

Essential Exam Tips

☑ Don't spend ages agonising over an introduction. An introduction can provide a clear overview and help give you a starting point but it's not worth spending lots of time on.

☑ You can't write about everything in the extract so choose words and phrases from the extract that you understand! If you choose a line that you are not sure about, this can lead to a very muddled response.

The use of **paradox** shows how the witches blur the lines between appearance and reality, tricking the characters.

The **'gory'** ghost adds enormous **dramatic tension**. It is perhaps a manifestation of Macbeth's guilty conscience rather than a spirit from the afterlife.

'Fair is foul and foul is fair'

'Enter the ghost of Banquo '

The witches open the play with a deliberate sense of confusion.

The supernatural is also evident through the ghost of Banquo.

Supernatural

The witches trick Macbeth and he only realises this at the end.

Do the witches completely control the Macbeths?

'juggling fiends'

Yes: They send the dagger to guide Macbeth to kill King Duncan.

This is Macbeth's moment of **anagnorisis**, when he realises that the witches have been playing with him; he can do nothing but fight to his death.

No: The dagger is a manifestation of Macbeth's own guilt and he is in control of his own decision-making.

Read the following extract from Act1 Scene 3 of 'Macbeth'.
Answer both questions below the text.

At this point in the play, Macbeth meets the witches for the first time.

ALL:
The weird sisters, hand in hand,
Posters of the sea and land,
Thus do go about, about:
Thrice to thine and thrice to mine
And thrice again, to make up nine.
Peace! the charm's wound up.

ENTER MACBETH AND BANQUO

MACBETH:
So foul and fair a day I have not seen.

BANQUO:
How far is't call'd to Forres? What are these
So wither'd and so wild in their attire,
That look not like the inhabitants o' the earth,
And yet are on't? Live you? or are you aught
That man may question? You seem to understand me,
By each at once her chappy finger laying
Upon her skinny lips: you should be women,
And yet your beards forbid me to interpret
That you are so.

a) Discuss how the supernatural is presented in this extract.

b) Discuss how the supernatural is presented in the play as a whole.

 Start with an overview

The supernatural is at the heart of the play, influencing the characters and creating gripping dramatic tension. In the extract, the witches meet Macbeth yet this is no coincidence; in Act One Scene One, they planned to do this, showing the audience just how much power they exert over the action of the play.

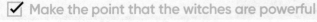 **Make the point that the witches are powerful**

In this scene, the witches speak mainly in lines of seven syllables in clear ***contrast*** to the ***iambic pentameter*** of the highborn lords. Shakespeare uses this ***rhythm*** to orally separate the witches from the human world and to create a sense of their power in their ***rhythmic*** chanting. This is enhanced by the ***rhyming couplets*** that they use and also the united front that they present. They are **'hand in hand'** which suggests they are working together while their own definition of themselves as **'sisters'** also suggests strong bonds between them. Their combined power is formidable and we are left in no doubt at the end that they have created a potent spell with **'the charm's wound up'**. The ***monosyllabic*** words here emphasise the sense of power and certainty, and tension sharply rises as Macbeth enters and the audience remembers that the witches have planned this meeting in the opening scene.

✓ Move to the point that the witches can influence the characters

When the witches complete their spell, **'thrice'** (three) is **repeated** to complete the spell of making the three prophecies (Glamis/Cawdor/King) that will convince Macbeth to kill the king. **'Three'** was a number associated with magic in Jacobean times so the audience would have known magic was at work. Shakespeare is perhaps referencing the Fates in Greek mythology, the three sisters who controlled the fate of men. He makes the connection to show us how much power the witches have over Macbeth, influencing him so that he allows his ambition to overrule him. Macbeth is clearly already under the influence of the witches as his opening words in the play here **'so foul and fair a day I have not seen'** echo the witches' words in Act 1 Scene 1 with **'fair is foul and foul is fair'**, showing how they are already controlling him. The use of **paradox** here reminds the audience that the witches cannot be trusted yet Macbeth's ambition blinds him to this.

✓ Make the point that the witches' aim is to create confusion in the world of men

Banquo's response to the sight of the witches captures his confusion. His many **questions** show he cannot rationalise (undertand) them; they are **'women'** yet have **'beards'** and this emphasises the theme of appearance and reality established from the beginning. It is the witches' purpose to create disorder through tricking men and this is seen in the opening scene which opens with the **'thunder and lightning'** that reflects a disturbance in nature. The **pathetic fallacy** warns the audience that a troubled time is coming. The Jacobean audience believed that disruption in nature (the macrocosm) reflected the human world (microcosm); Shakespeare uses the disturbance in nature to **symbolise** the potential disruption in the world of men. This, with the witches' presence, would have created a sense of deep unease from the opening moments.

✓ Explore how the supernatural destroys both Macbeth and Lady Macbeth

Later in the play, the witches state that the apparitions in Act 4 are true predictions, that **'all this is so'** and that their words speak the truth. The simple, **monosyllabic** statement of certainty shows utter conviction and **structurally,** the next scene take us to the murder of Macduff's family to illustrate how quickly Macbeth acts on the witches' apparitions, completely convinced in their accuracy. However, it is ironic that, by trying to eliminate Macduff as a threat, Macbeth ensures Macduff's anger and revenge that will end in Macbeth's death. It is only right at the end that Macbeth understands that he has been completely deceived by the **'juggling fiends'** as his **anagnorisis** comes when Macduff reveals that he has born by Caesarean section and can therefore kill Macbeth. By then, it is too late and Macbeth cannot do anything but fight to the death. Lady Macbeth is also destroyed by the supernatural as she is driven mad by her visions of blood, crying **'out damned spot'.** These visions could be sent by the evil spirits she once freely turned to in order to torment her and lead her to suicide.

✓ Explore whether the witches have complete control over the actions of the characters

It seems as if the witches do exert enormous power, weaving their spells throughout the play to toy with Macbeth and send him to his doom. An example of this in when the witches send the dagger in Act 2 to **'marshall'st'** Macbeth towards King Duncan's chamber. Macbeth might yet have decided against killing Duncan if the dagger had not guided him at this crucial time. The Jacobeans believed in predetermination which is the philosophy that everything in life is mapped out for us by God or fate; perhaps the vision of the dagger is the witches' way of ensuring that Macbeth follows his alloted path. However, Shakespeare was interested in the idea of self-determination, the way in which people control their own lives., and it is possible that.the dagger is simply a manifestation of Macbeth's own guilt. As the vision fades, he admits that **'there's no such thing'** and then with absolute purpose walks with his dagger to Duncan's chamber. He seems to be in control of his own actions. Yet even if the witches' actual power is ambiguous, it is very clear that the presence of the supernatural in the play creates constant **dramatic tension** which leaves any audience chilled.

Macbeth and Lady Macbeth work together to kill the king yet this close relationship breaks down under the weight of their crime.

'my dearest partner in greatness'	• Macbeth addresses Lady Macbeth in his letter. • The **superlative 'dearest'** shows the love that he has for his wife. **'Partner'** suggests an equal, loving relationship. • The word **'greatness'** refers to the ambition that already lies in them both.

'Come, you spirits...come'

• Lady Macbeth clearly knows her husband well; she knows that he might be **'too full o' the milk of human kindness'** to commit murder. Fearing what she sees as Macbeth's human weakness, Lady Macbeth asks the supernatural forces to unsex her so that she can be stronger and more powerful.

• The use of the **imperative verb 'come'** shows that she deliberately turns to the forces of evil and welcomes them in. Lady Macbeth is established as a woman in control of her relationship and her life.

• The **repetition** of **'come'** makes it sound as if she is casting a spell, and therefore her language links her with the witches.

Context: The Jacobean audience were highly superstitious and would have believed in the power of the supernatural. It was also a patriarchal society; for Lady Macbeth to take control in this way was highly unusual and would have been seen as unnatural.

'Look like the innocent flower/ But be the serpent under't'

- Lady Macbeth urges Macbeth to deceive everyone as they plan the king's murder; she is the one to corrupt him.

- The *enjambment* and the turning point of the word **'but'** highlight the deliberate slyness and the *contrast* between outward appearance and the inner reality. Lady Macbeth is adept at manipulating her husband.

Context: The *imagery* reminds the church-going Jacobean audience of the serpent in the Garden of Eden as Lady Macbeth's language links her to the weak woman who tempted Adam to disobey God. Shakespeare shows her as manipulative and sinful, reflecting contemporary stereotypes.

'Go get some water and wash this filthy witness from your hand'

- Lady Macbeth orders her husband to wash the blood off his hands.

- The *imperative verb* **'go'** reflects her control of her husband and the situation. As Macbeth is overwhelmed by guilt, she is more practical. She shows contempt for him in her brusque commands.

- Yet the commands might not indicate contempt; they might reflect her desperation to hide all evidence and her desire to protect her husband.

'Be innocent of the knowledge, dearest chuck'

- After becoming king, Macbeth begins to confide less and less in his wife, planning the murders of Banquo and Fleance on his own.

- The *superlative adjective* **'dearest'** reminds us of how he first addresses her as **'dearest partner'**, suggesting that his love is as strong as ever. His desire to keep her innocent could be a desire to protect her.

- Yet she is not now a **'partner'** but is a **'chuck'**. This perhaps shows that he no longer values her as highly as he did. **'Chuck'** means a senseless chicken; perhaps it is a term of endearment but it does not suggest the same status that **'partner'** does.

'Are you a man?'

- At the feast, Banquo's ghost makes Macbeth flinch in fear and causes Lady Macbeth to try to calm him and bring him to reality.

- Her use of the question is a direct challenge, and the blunt *monosyllables* help reflect her anxiety at Macbeth's behaviour.

- In Act 1, appealing to Macbeth's manhood worked; in Act 3, it does not and the feast is dispersed. Lady Macbeth is losing her influence over her husband.

'she should have died hereafter'

- When he hears news of his wife's suicide, Macbeth dismisses her death in one sentence.

- This could perhaps show his callousness (lack of emotion) which suggests his brutal killing spree has stripped him of human qualities and he is now more monster than man; his love for his wife is eroded.

- However, it could suggest a pain at her death; certainly he looks ahead at his future without her as empty and tedious, saying **'to-morrow, and to-morrow, and to-morrow/Creeps in this petty pace'**. The ***repetition*** shows a dreary weariness and the time ***metaphor*** reflects the monotony of his last moments on earth without his partner.

Grade 9 Exploration:
Look at the relationship in a different way

Within the relationship, who is most to blame for Duncan's murder?

Macbeth: Macbeth is the one who commits the ultimate betrayal of regicide. His subsequent murders of Banquo and Macduff's family, planned on his own and not with his wife, show how his **'vaulting ambition'** is his great motivation and how he chooses his own disastrous destiny. The patriarchal society that Shakespeare was writing in also meant that Macbeth would have been in a position of power and authority over his wife; he cannot blame her for his actions.

Lady Macbeth: A Jacobean audience would have been repelled by Lady Macbeth's turning to the evil spirits to give her unnatural strength. Her deliberate and relentless control of her husband reflects back to the Bible's Book of Genesis which established women as wily manipulators through Eve's temptation of Adam.

Regicide (killing of a king/queen) was seen as an appalling crime because it was a sin against God. The Jacobeans believed in the divine right of kings, that God anointed (chose) the monarch, and both of their parts in such a crime would have been viewed as unforgivable.

The *superlative* **'dearest'** shows the love that he has for his wife. **'Partner'** suggests an equal, loving relationship.

The *enjambment* and the turning point of the word **'but'** highlight the deliberate slyness and the contrast between outward appearance and the inner reality.

'my dearest partner in greatness'

'Look like the innocent flower/But be the serpent under't'

Macbeth and Lady Macbeth are close.

Lady Macbeth manipulates her husband.

Lord & Lady Macbeth

Guilt destroys their relationship.

Who is most to blame within the relationship for Scotland's bloodshed?

'She should have died hereafter'

Macbeth: Many of his crimes are committed on his own due to his 'vaulting ambition'. He chooses his own disastrous destiny.

Tormented by guilt, Lady Macbeth kills herself and Macbeth reacts with despair, his life empty of meaning without her.

Lady Macbeth: Lady Macbeth urges her husband to commit the first murder, relentlessly manipulating him.

Read the following extract from Act 1 Scene 7 of 'Macbeth'. Answer both questions below the text.

At this point in the play, Macbeth has just decided not to kill Duncan.

MACBETH:
Prithee, peace.
I dare do all that may become a man;
Who dares do more is none.

LADY MACBETH:
What beast was't, then,
That made you break this enterprise to me?
When you durst do it, then you were a man;
And, to be more than what you were, you would
Be so much more the man. Nor time nor place
Did then adhere, and yet you would make both:
They have made themselves, and that their fitness now
Does unmake you. I have given suck, and know
How tender 'tis to love the babe that milks me:
I would, while it was smiling in my face,
Have pluck'd my nipple from his boneless gums,
And dash'd the brains out, had I so sworn as you
Have done to this.

MACBETH:
If we should fail?

LADY MACBETH:
We fail!
But screw your courage to the sticking-place,
And we'll not fail.

a) Explore how the Macbeths' relationship is presented in this extract.

b) Explore how their relationship is presented in the play as a whole.

 Start with an overview

Macbeth and Lady Macbeth begin the play as close partners yet their relationship comes under huge strain. In the extract, Lady Macbeth manipulates her husband into committing to kill King Duncan; we wonder if she would be so passionate and so persuasive if she could look into the future and see how her relationship will be destroyed by the decisions that they take.

 Make the point that Macbeth seems to be in control at first but this soon changes

In the extract, Macbeth has clearly decided that he will not commit the great crime of killing the king, saying **'I dare do all that may become a man; Who dares do more is none.'** He understands that killing the king will completely change him and that regicide is not the action of a heroic brave soldier, that it will unman him.

Regicide was seen as an appalling crime in Jacobean times as it was a sin against God, and Macbeth's sense of nobility is clear here. His dismissive **'prithee, peace'** seeks to silence his wife as he would, in that patriarchal society, have been in a position of autonomy (power) over her. Yet Lady Macbeth is not silenced as her long impassioned speech shows. She proves herself to be an expert manipulator, playing on Macbeth's sense of masculinity with the words **'when you durst do it, then you were a man'**. She is suggesting that he is not brave enough, not man enough, to commit to killing Duncan, but Shakespeare is showing us that her version of manhood is just someone without morality.

✓ Develop the point about how Lady Macbeth controls her husband

Lady Macbeth tells her husband that she would rather kill her own child than be the coward that he is. She refers to a baby that she **'gave suck'** to, quite probably referring to their dead son although this is not explicit. By using such a painful subject, she plays on Macbeth's emotions about this shared memory and continues to do so as she describes how she would have **'pluck'd my nipple from his boneless gums/And dash'd the brains out'**. Ambition has stripped her of all feminine qualities. The viciousness of this *image* is a potent one; the *verb* **'pluck'd'** is *onomatopoeic* which emphasises the violence with which Lady Macbeth is speaking. The Jacobean audience believed that women were natural nurturers and Lady Macbeth's *vocabulary* would have been shocking to a contemporary audience as it is so unnatural.

✓ Move on to show how Macbeth and Lady Macbeth are clearly close

There is a sense of closeness in the *sentence structure* of Macbeth's **'if we should fail'** and Lady Macbeth's **'we fail!'** The way she picks up on his words and uses them herself show a sense of comradeship and closeness. This is seen from the beginning when Macbeth writes a letter about the witches' predictions to **'my dearest partner in greatness'.** The address is interesing as **'partner'** suggests an equal, loving relationship. This closeness is enhanced by the *superlative* **'dearest'** while the *noun* **'greatness'** suggests the ambition that already lies in them both. There is a shared hunger for power that cements their relationship yet ultimately destroys it.

✓ Explore how their relationship changes

After becoming king, Macbeth begins to confide less in his wife, planning the murders of Banquo and Fleance on his own and telling Lady Macbeth to **'be innocent of the knowledge, dearest chuck'** .The *superlative adjective* **'dearest'** reminds us of how he first addresses her as **'dearest partner'**, suggesting his love is as strong as ever. His desire to keep her innocent could be a desire to protect her. Yet she is not now a **'partner'** but is a **'chuck',** perhaps showing that he no longer values her as highly as he did. **'Chuck'** means a senseless chicken; perhaps it is a term of endearment but it does not suggest the same status that **'partner'** does. Later, at the feast, Banquo's ghost makes Macbeth flinch in fear and causes Lady Macbeth to try to calm him and bring him to reality, hissing **'are you a man?'** Her use of the question is a direct challenge, and the blunt *monosyllables* help reflect her anxiety at Macbeth's behaviour. In Act 1, appealing to Macbeth's manhood worked; in Act 3, it does not and the feast is dispersed, reflecting the fact that Lady Macbeth is losing her influence over her husband.

✓ Explore whether there is any love left between them at the end

At the end, Lady Macbeth's mind has been broken by her guilt which has consumed her so that not even her love for her husband and her desire for power can make her life bearable, and she kills herself. There is ambiguity in Macbeth's response to his wife's death: **'she should have died hereafter'**. Where once she was his **'dearest partner in greatness'**, here he dismisses her death in one sentence. This could perhaps show his callousness (lack of emotion) which suggests his brutal killing spree has stripped him of human qualities and he is now more monster than man. However, it could suggest a pain at her death; certainly he looks ahead at his future without her as empty and tedious. The *repetition* in his lines **'to-morrow, and to-morrow, and to-morrow'** shows a dreary weariness and the time *metaphor* reflects the monotony of his last moments on earth. The *verb* **'creeps in this petty pace'** stresses how slowly the time passes as he contemplates a future without his wife. By the end of the play, we see the Macbeths paying the price of their crime; the Jacobean audience would have viewed their parts in such a crime as unforgivable as regicide was viewed as a sin against God. 'Macbeth' is a play about power and ambition yet it also documents the breakdown of a relationship.

One of the questions raised by the play is whether Macbeth had any control over his actions or whether he simply followed fate's path.

'fair is foul and foul is fair'

- The witches create a sense of confusion, upsetting the world of men. Their spells deliberately control Macbeth's actions.

- The use of **paradox** here highlights the power of the witches; they will give Macbeth **'fair'** prophecies yet these will end up with **'foul'** consequences. The **repetition** of the **'f'** sounds emphasises a sense of forceful power and the **monosyllabic** words enhance the sense of the chanting of a spell.

- We remember this spell when Macbeth says **'so fair and foul a day'**, immediately linking him with the forces of evil and implying that he is already being influenced by the spell that they have made.

Context: The Jacobean audience was superstitious, firmly believing in the presence and power of witches. They would have believed that the witches had the ability to control Macbeth.

'chance may crown me without my stir'

- Macbeth considers the witches' predictions and initially decides to let fate control events.

- Yet even as he says this, Banquo comments on how **'rapt'** (absorbed) Macbeth is, leaving us aware that he may well change his mind and **'stir'** himself to action. This awareness contributes to the **dramatic tension** as we wonder whether Macbeth will take action and control events.

'When you durst do it, then you were a man'

- Lady Macbeth uses ideas of manhood to manipulate her husband into killing Duncan, suggesting that he is not brave enough.

- Macbeth is pressurised by his wife, making us wonder just much much free will he has.

Context: Jacobean society was a patriarchal one which meant that men held authority over their wives. Macbeth is led by his wife but he has the power at any time to resist her strategies.

'I have no spur... but only vaulting ambition... which o'er leaps itself'	• The horse **metaphor** shows his ambition to be incredibly powerful. Macbeth already knows that his ambition could lead to disaster as it loses control and **'o'er leaps itself'** yet he still chooses to murder his king. It is his choice to act to fulfil his ambition that sets the tragedy into motion.	**Context:** Shakespeare uses the Greek tragedy convention of a tragic and noble hero who has a fatal flaw or weakness: a **hamartia** which leads to his downfall. Macbeth's **hamartia** is his ambition.
'I see thee... I see thee still... with gouts of blood... there's no such thing'	• Macbeth experiences a hallucination of a bloody dagger, guiding him towards the king's chamber. The hallucination represents his guilt; he knows that what he plans is terribly wrong.	**Context:** Shakespearean theatre would have been limited in terms of props/ special effects so the hideous vocabulary of **'gouts of blood'** works hard to help the audience imagine the violent murder.
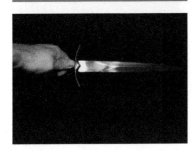	• The **structure** of the lines suggests that Macbeth is scattered, unsettled, as even at this point he is unsure as to whether he will commit the crime of murder. This increases our tension as we watch and wonder but, by the end of the **soliloquy**, he has made up his mind and turns to Duncan's chamber. • An alternative reading is that the witches send the dagger to lead Macbeth to kill Duncan. Macbeth follows it, helpless to resist.	
'Come Fate into the list... champion me'	• Macbeth is determined to hold onto his crown and to defy the witches' prophecy that Banquo's children will become kings. • He calls for fate to fight on his behalf. Of course, fate ignores him. • The **imperative verb** 'come' shows his decisiveness as he challenges fate to help him alter Scotland's destiny.	**Context:** The imagery of jousting shows his combative nature, his soldier's spirit and it also references the popular 17th century sport.

'Life's but a walking shadow, a poor player'

- Macbeth's last **soliloquy** reveals his thoughts after he hears the news of Lady Macbeth's death, just before his last battle.

- The **tone** is depressed and resigned as he reflects on the meaning of life. The theatre **metaphor** suggests that we are all merely actors playing out a preplanned script.

- The **plosive** sounds of '**poor player**' reveal the bitterness as Macbeth realises that he has lost and his ambition has come to nothing. Fate has led him to his heart's desire yet it has not brought him any happiness.

Grade 9 Exploration:
Look at the theme in a different way

Do the characters have any free choice in their actions or does fate decide it all?

Fate: The power of fate is clear. Even though Macbeth tries to change the course of events, Banquo's sons still eventually inherit the throne of Scotland. The three witches represent the three Fates, sisters in Greek mythology who controlled men's destinies, and their power in controlling Macbeth is seen throughout the play.

Free Will: Macbeth had many chances to turn from his evil path yet does not choose to do this. He is in control of his destiny throughout; if anything, it is his own fatal flaw of ambition that controls him.

The Jacobeans believed in predetermination, the belief that our lives are planned out before we are born, but Shakespeare was interested in the idea of self-determination, the way in which people control their own lives. This exploration is evident in the examination of fate's role in the play; does it control us or do we make our own decisions?

Essential Exam Tips

☑ Aim for five detailed paragraphs; your response will be evaluated on quality not quantity but it's difficult to make your response good if it is too brief.

☑ Most of the exam boards require you to write about context.
Check whether your exam board gives marks for this and, if it does, make sure you weave points about Shakespeare's audience and literary conventions into your response.

Macbeth's opening words echo the witches', showing how they are already influencing him.

He chooses to murder his king, demonstrating clear free will. It is his ambition that sets the tragedy into motion.

'fair is foul and foul is fair'

'vaulting ambition'

The witches control Macbeth with their spells.

Macbeth allows his ambition to guide his actions.

Fate & Free Will

Macbeth tries to change destiny by asking fate to help him.

Do the characters have any control over their actions?

'Come Fate into the list'

Yes: Macbeth has many chances to turn from his evil path yet does not choose to do this.

He is unsuccessful, demonstrating the pointlessness of challenging or trying to change fate.

No: The power of fate is clear. Even though Macbeth tries to change the course of events, Banquo's sons will still eventually inherit the throne of Scotland.

Sample GCSE Exam Question

Read the following extract from Act 1 Scene 3 of 'Macbeth'.
Answer both questions below the text.

At this point in the play, Macbeth considers the witches' prophecies.

MACBETH:
[Aside] Two truths are told,
As happy prologues to the swelling act
Of the imperial theme. – I thank you, gentlemen.
[Aside] This supernatural soliciting
Cannot be ill, cannot be good: if ill,
Why hath it given me earnest of success,
Commencing in a truth? I am thane of Cawdor:
If good, why do I yield to that suggestion
Whose horrid image doth unfix my hair
And make my seated heart knock at my ribs,
Against the use of nature? Present fears
Are less than horrible imaginings:
My thought, whose murder yet is but fantastical,
Shakes so my single state of man
That function is smother'd in surmise
And nothing is but what is not.

a) Discuss how ideas of fate and free will are presented in this extract.

b) Discuss how these ideas are presented in the play as a whole.

 # Sample GCSE Answer

 Start with an overview

One of the questions raised by the play is whether Macbeth had any control over his actions or whether he simply followed fate's path. At this point in the play, he has just heard the witches' prophecies and contemplates them, wondering whether he should act on them or allow fate to run its course.

 Make the point that Macbeth seems to have no free will as he is controlled by the witches

This is the first point in the play that we hear Macbeth's honest responses to the witches' predictions and as such it is dramatically tense. Through Macbeth's private asides, Shakespeare allows the audience to see the inner workings of his mind. There is already great uncertainty; the **repetitive sentence structure** of the phrase **'cannot be ill, cannot be good'** show the ambiguity with which he receives the predictions. He is uncertain and with that uncertainty comes indecision; should he act on the prophecies or not? This uncertainty is deliberately created by the witches, whose power to blur appearance and reality is formidable. Their words **'fair is foul and foul is fair'** use ***paradox*** to create a sense of confusion; they will give him **'fair'** prophecies yet these will end up with **'foul'** consequences. The ***repetition*** of the **'f'** sounds emphasises a sense of forceful power and the ***monosyllabic*** words enhance the sense of the chanting of a spell. The Jacobean audience was superstitious, firmly believing in the presence and power of witches. They would have believed that the spell controlled Macbeth and his actions, allowing him no free will.

✓ Move to the point that Macbeth begins to consider how to influence Fate

Macbeth is already thinking of murder; he speaks of the **'horrid image doth unfix my hair/And make my seated heart knock at my ribs/Against the use of nature'**. The language clearly reflects the enormity of the action he is planning; his entire body is reacting dramatically and unnaturally to the thought of murdering Duncan. Regicide was viewed as an unnatural act against God by Jacobean audiences and Macbeth's physical reaction is an understandably violent one. Even though it might be his fate to become king, Macbeth is clearly considering ways to speed events up and to allow no room for error. This thought terrifies him.

✓ Move to the point that Macbeth does begin to make decisions

Macbeth ends his musings by deciding to let fate control events, saying **'if chance will have me king, why, chance may crown me, without my stir'**. Yet even as he says this, Banquo comments on how **'rapt'** (absorbed) Macbeth is, leaving the audience aware that he may well change his mind and **'stir'** himself to action. This awareness contributes to the *dramatic tension* of the scene. And soon enough, Macbeth does begin to consider action as his ambition starts to motivate him. Later, he admits **'I have no spur... but only vaulting ambition... which o'er leaps itself'** and the horse *metaphor* shows his ambition to be incredibly powerful. Macbeth already knows that his ambition could lead to disaster as it loses control and **'o'er leaps itself'** yet he still chooses to murder his king. It is his ambition that sets the tragedy into motion. Shakespeare uses the Greek tragedy convention of a tragic and noble hero who has a fatal flaw (weakness), a *hamartia* which leads to his downfall. Macbeth's *hamartia* is his ambition which prompts him to commit dreadful acts.

✓ Move on to show how Macbeth's actions have no impact on the power of fate

Macbeth is determined to hold onto his crown and to defy the witches' prophecy that Banquo's children will become kings. Later, he calls for fate to fight on his behalf, saying **'Come Fate into the list... champion me'** and using the **imagery** of jousting which shows his combative nature and also references the popular 17th century sport. The *imperative verb* **'come'** shows his decisiveness as he challenges Scotland's destiny. Yet it is all for nothing and fate cannot be changed despite Macbeth's brutal actions to alter destiny. Macbeth's last *soliloquy* reveals his thoughts after he hears the news of Lady Macbeth's death, just before his last battle, and says **'life's but a walking shadow, a poor player'**. The *tone* is depressed and resigned as he reflects on the meaning of life. The theatre *metaphor* suggests that we are merely actors playing out a pre-planned script and the *plosive* sounds of **'poor player'** reveal the bitterness as Macbeth realises that he has lost and his ambition has come to nothing. Fate has led him to his heart's desire yet it has not brought him any happiness.

✓ Explore whether the characters have any free choice in their actions or whether Fate decides it all

The power of fate is clear. Even though Macbeth tries to change the course of events, Banquo's sons will still eventually inherit the throne of Scotland. The three witches represent the three Fates, sisters in Greek mythology who controlled men's destinies, and their power in controlling Macbeth is seen throughout the play. However, Macbeth had many chances to turn from his evil path yet does not choose to do this. He is in control of his destiny throughout; if anything, it is his own fatal flaw of ambition that controls him. The Jacobeans believed in predetermination but Shakespeare was interested in the idea of self-determination, the way in which people control their own lives. This exploration is evident in the examination of fate's role in the play. It is one of the ongoing questions that 'Macbeth' prompts and makes us, even four hundred years later, wonder just how much autonomy we have over our lives.

9 Ambition

Exploration of a theme

The power and the dangers of ambition are constantly explored in 'Macbeth' as the plot revolves around the decision to kill for power and the consequences of this decision.

'Hail to thee, Glamis/Cawdor/ King hereafter'

- The witches give Macbeth their predictions, each reflecting rising status with the king being the last and most powerful title.

- The witches' intention is to disrupt the world of men. We wonder whether the witches create a spell that controls a helpless Macbeth or whether their prophecies merely spark Macbeth's ambition.

Context: The Jacobeans believed in predetermination but Shakespeare was interested in the idea of self-determination, the way in which people control their own lives. This exploration is evident in the examination of the witches' role in the play; do they control the characters or do the characters have autonomy over their decision-making? Is Macbeth to blame for his ambition?

'Stars, hide your fires; Let not light see my black and deep desires'

- Macbeth hears Duncan announce that his son Malcolm will inherit the crown and immediately Macbeth sees this as an obstacle to his own ambition.

- **Structurally,** we see how swiftly Macbeth's ambition has grown. He is not content to let fate run its course and to see whether he naturally becomes king; already he is planning murder. The heavy **alliteration** of the **'d'** consonants in **'deep desires'** shows his evil intentions.

- The **imagery** of blocked out light and working in darkness reflects the sinister path that Macbeth's ambition is taking him down.

'I have no spur... but only vaulting ambition... which o'er leaps itself'

- Macbeth is fully aware that his ambition is the only motivation to kill the king.

- The horse **metaphor** shows his ambition to be incredibly powerful. Macbeth already knows that his ambition could lead to disaster as it loses control and **'o'er leaps itself'**; however, he still chooses to murder his king.

Context: Shakespeare uses the Greek tragedy convention of a tragic and noble hero who has a fatal flaw (weakness)- a hamartia which leads to his downfall. Macbeth's **hamartia** is his ambition.

'Come, you spirits... come'

- Lady Macbeth turns to the forces of evil and welcomes the dark spirits who will strip her of her femininity and allow her to commit murder and seize power.

- The use of the **imperative verb 'come'** shows that her ambition is so strong that she deliberately turns to the forces of evil and welcomes them in.

Context: The Jacobean audience believed that women were natural nurturers, meek and subservient. Lady Macbeth's decision to unsex herself to fulfil her desire for power would have been viewed as shocking to a Jacobean audience.

'I dreamt last night of the three weird sisters'

- Banquo's words illustrate how he is still brooding on the predictions that his sons will be kings of Scotland.

- His open admission of how the witches have stayed on his mind is a direct **contrast** to Macbeth's lie **'I think not of them'**.

- Banquo is clearly a man of some ambition- like Macbeth. Yet Banquo does not act on this ambition. Shakespeare uses him as a **foil** (contrast) to Macbeth, who does act on it.

'I could not say 'Amen''

- Immediately after the regicide, Macbeth is consumed with guilt and is unable to say the traditional response to a religious blessing. His actions have placed him beyond God's love and comfort and his ambition has brought him mental anguish. **Structurally**, this is effective as it illustrates how quickly the guilt takes hold of Macbeth, showing how his ambition has taken him down a terrible path of mental torment.

Context: Regicide was seen as an appalling crime because it was a sin against God. The audience would understand the sacrilegious nature of Macbeth's crime and condemn the ambition that has motivated him to such evil.

'give to the edge o' the sword/his wife, his babes'	• Macbeth's desire for complete power leads him to despicable acts such as the murder of Macduff's family.
	• The *imperative verb* captures his cold-hearted sense of purpose and the use of **'babes'**, *symbol* of innocence, illustrates that Macbeth is fully aware of what he is ordering.
	• Ambition has stripped Macbeth of all compassion; he is now more monster than man.

'Out damned spot'	• As her mind collapses into madness, Lady Macbeth sees visions of blood.
	• Her ambition has brought her no happiness and the play documents the disintegration of her mind, her power and her relationship with her husband as a consequence of her ambition.
	• Her *fragmented, unstructured speech* shows her at the very end as weak and broken, crippled by her ambition.

Grade 9 Exploration:
Look at the theme in a different way

Has all ambition been extinguished by the end of the play?

Yes: Shakespeare uses the classic five act play *structure* of the ancient Greeks which always ended with *resolution*. With Macbeth dead, Malcolm, the rightful heir, takes the crown and there is a sense of closure at the end. The audience is reassured that the ambition which has thrown Scotland into bloody war is now purged and lessons about the dangers of ambition have been learnt. The play ends with peace and order.

No: The audience is uneasily aware that the prophecy of Banquo's children becoming kings has yet to come to pass. We wonder whether Fleance, Banquo's son, will also become motivated by powerful ambition and whether the peace in Scotland will last. The cyclical *structure* of the play- the play starts and ends with the death of a traitor after civil war- reinforces this sense that Scotland is doomed to repeat the same pattern of **'vaulting ambition'**. Shakespeare explores human nature and the ambition that lies in all of us; perhaps Shakespeare is asking us to consider how far we would go to fulfil our own **'black and deep desires'**.

✎ Essential Exam Tip

☑ Shakespeare does not use many stage directions; if they are used, do see if you can comment on them. Stage directions form part of Shakespeare's dramatic techniques so do analyse them if you can.

The horse *metaphor* shows his ambition as incredibly powerful. Ambition is Macbeth's fatal flaw or *hamartia*.

The *imagery* of blocked out light and working in darkness reflects the sinister path that Macbeth's ambition is taking him.

'I have no spur... but only vaulting ambition... which o'er leaps itself'

'Stars, hide your fires; let not light see my black and deep desires'

Ambition is Macbeth's only motivation.

Ambition and the desire for power are seen as negative.

Ambition

Ambition brings disaster and unhappiness.

Has ambition been extinguished by the end of the play?

'I could not say 'Amen'

Yes: With Malcolm as king, the audience is reassured that the ambition is now purged and lessons about the dangers of ambition have been learnt.

Macbeth knows that he will not sleep again; his conscience will be always tormented by his actions.

No: The audience is uneasily aware that the prophecy of Banquo's children becoming kings has yet to happen. Will Fleance also fall prey to ambition?

Sample GCSE Exam Question

Read the following extract from Act 1 Scene 7 of 'Macbeth'. Answer both questions below the text.

At this point in the play, Macbeth is deliberating over whether to kill King Duncan.

MACBETH:
He's here in double trust;
First, as I am his kinsman and his subject,
Strong both against the deed; then, as his host,
Who should against his murderer shut the door,
Not bear the knife myself. Besides, this Duncan
Hath borne his faculties so meek, hath been
So clear in his great office, that his virtues
Will plead like angels, trumpet-tongued, against
The deep damnation of his taking-off;
And pity, like a naked new-born babe,
Striding the blast, or heaven's cherubim, horsed
Upon the sightless couriers of the air,
Shall blow the horrid deed in every eye,
That tears shall drown the wind. I have no spur
To prick the sides of my intent, but only
Vaulting ambition, which o'erleaps itself
And falls on the other.

a) How are ideas about ambition portrayed in this extract?
b) How are ideas about ambition portrayed in the play as a whole?

Sample GCSE Answer

☑ **Start with an overview**

The power and the dangers of ambition are constantly explored in 'Macbeth' as the plot revolves around the decision to kill for power and the consequences of this decision. In the extract, Macbeth acknowledges the power of the ambition that drives him and the audience watches him struggle with his conscience, wondering which will prove stronger: ambition or morality.

☑ **Make the point that Macbeth is clearly ambitious**

In the extract, Shakespeare gives Macbeth a **soliloquy** here to allow the audience to understand the emotions and impulses that drive him, and his last sentence leaves us in no doubt as to what his main motivator is. He admits to himself that **'I have no spur/To prick the sides of my intent, but only/Vaulting ambition, which o'erleaps itself/And falls on the other'**. The horse **metaphor** establishes his ambition as incredibly powerful and that Macbeth already knows that his ambition could lead to disaster as it loses control and **'o'er leaps itself'** yet he is still tempted. Shakespeare uses the Greek tragedy convention of a tragic and noble hero who has a fatal flaw (weakness), a **hamartia**, which leads to his downfall. Macbeth's **hamartia** is his ambition. The strength of this ambition is seen as Macbeth considers the solid reasons why he should not harm his king, acknowledging that Macbeth is Duncan's **'kinsman and his subject'**. The Jacobeans considered family loyalty to be incredibly important while the notion of absolute loyalty to the monarch was embedded in the idea of the divine right of kings. This idea meant that the Jacobeans believed that the monarch was chosen by God and therefore should be revered, respected and protected as a religious obligation. Macbeth feels these ties strongly, as well as the tie of his position of **'host'**, yet such is the power of his ambition that he muses on his plan to ignore all these obligations and to kill the man who is his guest, family member and monarch.

✓ Move to the point that ambition corrupts people

This negative impact of ambition continues to be shown as Macbeth broods on just how terrible the act is that his ambition is tempting him to carry out, calling it a **'horrid deed'** that will cause such outrage among the people that their **'tears shall drown the wind'**. The *image* of grief captures how dreadful the considered murder is, especially for a man who has a solid reputation as an honourable, brave soldier. Yet Macbeth is still tempted, propelled by the ambition that he knows will corrupt him. We see this when, earlier in the play, Macbeth hears Duncan announce that his son Malcolm will inherit the crown and immediately Macbeth sees this as an obstacle to his own ambition. ***Structurally***, we see how swiftly Macbeth's ambition has grown from the moment he received the witches' predictions. He is not content to let fate run its course and to see whether he naturally becomes king; already he is planning murder to fulfil his **'black and deep desires'**. The heavy ***alliteration*** of the **'d'** consonants here shows his evil intentions while the ***imagery*** of blocked out light and working in darkness reflects the sinister path that Macbeth's ambition is taking him down, and his full knowlege of this corrupting desire. Yet Shakespeare does use Banquo as an example of how ambition can be resisted. In Act 2, Banquo says **'I dreamt last night of the... weird sisters'**, showing he is a man of some ambition, like Macbeth. Yet Banquo does not act on this ambition and so Shakespeare uses him as a ***foil*** (contrast) to Macbeth, who does act on his ambition with such dreadful consequences.

✓ Continue to explore how ambition affects other characters

By the end of this extract, Macbeth is determined that the planned murder is too appalling, and tells Lady Macbeth that he will proceed no further with it. Yet even though he is suppressing his own ambition, he is no match for his wife's. Like Macbeth's, her ambition is sparked by the witches' propecies so that she sees the need to change herself in order to achieve her ambition, turning to the forces of evil and welcoming the dark spirits who will strip her of her femininity and allow her to commit murder as she says **'come, you spirits... come'**. The use of the ***imperative verb*** **'come'** shows just how determined she is. The Jacobean audience believed that women were natural nurturers, meek and subservient, and Lady Macbeth's decision to unsex herself to fulfil her desire for power would have been very shocking.

✓ Make the point that ambition does not bring happiness to the Macbeths

Immediately after the regicide, Macbeth is consumed with guilt and is unable to say the traditional response to a religious blessing, claiming **'I could not say 'Amen'**. His actions have placed him beyond God's love and comfort. ***Structurally***, this is effective as it illustrates how quickly the guilt takes hold of Macbeth, showing how his ambition has taken him down a terrible path. Similarly, the consequences of ambition drive Lady Macbeth mad as she rubs her hands of imaginary blood, saying **'out, damned spot'**. Her ambition has brought her no happiness and the play documents the disintegration of her mind, her power and her relationship with her husband as a consequence of her ambition.

✓ Explore whether ambition has been extinguished by the end of the play

Shakespeare uses the classic five act play ***structure*** of the ancient Greeks which always ended with ***resolution***. With Macbeth dead, Malcolm, the rightful heir, takes the crown and there is a sense of closure at the end. The audience is reassured that the ambition which has thrown Scotland into bloody war is now purged and lessons about the dangers of ambition have been learnt as the play ends with peace and order. Yet the audience is uneasily aware that the prophecy of Banquo's children becoming kings has yet to come to pass and we wonder whether Fleance, Banquo's son, will also become motivated by powerful ambition and whether the peace in Scotland will last. The play starts and ends with the death of a traitor after civil war, and this cyclical structure of the play reinforces this sense that Scotland is doomed to repeat the same pattern of events shaped by those with **'vaulting ambition'**. Shakespeare explores human nature and the ambition that lies in all of us. Perhaps Shakespeare is asking us to consider how far we would go to fulfil our own **'black and deep desires'**.

10 Appearance & Reality
Exploration of a theme

Lies and deceit lie at the heart of 'Macbeth'. In a world of **'fog and filthy air'**, it is not always easy to know who or what to trust, and Shakespeare explores this idea throughout the play.

'Fair is foul and foul is fair'

- The witches immediately create a sense of confusion, showing us that things are not always as they seem.

- The use of **paradox** here highlights the power of the witches; they will give Macbeth **'fair'** prophecies yet these will end up with **'foul'** consequences. The **repetition** of the **'f'** sounds emphasises a sense of forceful power and the **monosyllabic** words enhance the sense of the chanting of a spell; perhaps a spell to blur the lines between what is real and what is imagined, and therefore to create chaos.

- Shakespeare creates an atmosphere of malevolent (evil) power right at the beginning, establishing a world where nothing is as it seems, and is therefore dangerous.

'He was a gentleman on whom I built/An absolute trust'

- Duncan states how he completely trusted the traitor Cawdor.

- There is **dramatic irony** here as the **stage direction** immediately after these words signals Macbeth's entrance. The audience knows that Macbeth is already considering murdering the king, so tension is created when Duncan calls him **'worthiest cousin'**. The **superlative 'worthiest'** shows just how 'absolute' is the trust he holds for Macbeth, and only the audience know how wrong Duncan is to do so. We are aware that fair appearances deceive even those who are in positions of authority.

'Stars, hide your fires; Let not light see my black and deep desires'

- Macbeth hears Duncan announce that his son Malcolm will inherit the crown; immediately, Macbeth sees this as an obstacle to his own ambition, knowing that his ambition must be kept secret.

- Macbeth is already planning a murder so appalling that he cannot name it, referring instead ambiguously to his **'black and deep desires'**. The heavy **alliteration** here reinforces his evil intentions. The **imagery** of blocked out light and working in darkness emphasises how Macbeth must hide his terrible ambitions from the world.

'Look like the innocent flower/ but be the serpent under't'

- Lady Macbeth urges Macbeth to deceive everyone as they plan the king's murder.

- The **enjambment** and the turning point of the word **'but'** highlights the deliberate slyness and the **contrast** between outward appearance and the inner reality.

Context: The *imagery* reminds the church-going Jacobean audience of the serpent in the Garden of Eden as Lady Macbeth's language links her to the weak woman who tempted Adam to disobey God. Shakespeare presents her as manipulative and sinful, deliberately playing on contemporary perceptions of women as false and sly.

'I dreamt last night of the three weird sisters'

- Banquo's words reveal how he is still brooding on the predictions that his sons will be kings of Scotland.

- His open admission of how the witches have stayed on his mind is a direct **contrast** with Macbeth's lie **'I think not of them'**. The theme of appearance and reality is illustrated here through Banquo's open honest nature and Macbeth's deceit. Shakespeare uses him as a *foil* (contrast) to Macbeth.

'reconciled my thoughts/To thy good truth and honour'

- When Macduff comes to join Malcolm in England, Malcolm tests Macduff's loyalty by pretending to be evil. Macduff has passed the test and Malcolm's mind is now reassured as to Macduff's honourable intentions.

- Deceit here is used for good purposes; it is interesting that in this play even the characters aligned with good are forced to deceive.

- Malcolm shows himself as more cautious than his father, Duncan, who was too quick to put his **'absolute trust'** in others.

Context: The Jacobean audience lived in a world where betrayal and vying for power was common. They would approve of Malcolm's caution, which suggests that he will be a king who is shrewd and does not accept people on face value but will look closer at whether they are trustworthy.

'juggling fiends'

- Macbeth condemns the witches when Macduff reveals he has been born via Caesarean birth and can therefore kill Macbeth. He realises that he has been deceived.

- The *adjective* 'juggling' shows that he finally understands that the witches have been playing with him, tricking him and misleading him.

Context: *Anagnorisis* comes from the tradition of Greek theatre and is the moment where a character makes a critical discovery. Here, Macbeth realises that his faith in the witches has been misplaced; it is his moment of anagnorisis.

Grade 9 Exploration:
Look at the theme in a different way

Does the end of the play resolve the lies and deceits?

Yes: Shakespeare uses the classic five act play **structure** of the ancient Greeks which always ended with **resolution**. There is a sense of closure at the end of the play as the honest Malcolm promises in his statement that **'we will perform in measure, time and place'**, an intention to rule in a balanced and clear way. His sense of integrity is highlighted by the reference to his position as rightful king, ruling **'by the grace of Grace'** which reinforces his position as a king chosen by God. The audience is reassured that Scotland is now on course for a more open, harmonious period.

No: Shakespeare explores human nature and shows how deceit lies in all of us. The audience is uneasily aware that the prophecy of Banquo's children becoming kings has yet to come to pass. We wonder whether Fleance, Banquo's son, will also become motivated by powerful ambition which leads to deliberate dishonesty and which destroys peace. The play starts and ends with the death of a traitor after civil war, and this cyclical **structure** reinforces this sense that Scotland is doomed to repeat the same pattern, and that future generations will also create a world which will be based on falsehood and treachery.

✍ Essential Exam Tips

☑ When writing about themes, make sure you explain how the ideas affect the characters and also apply to the audience.

☑ Exam boards use different wording for the Shakespeare question. Check with your teacher or the exam board's website to see if you have to answer part a and part b separately OR whether you can weave the questions on the extract and the whole play together into one answer.

The *enjambment* and the turning point of the word **'but'** highlight the deliberate slyness and the contrast between outward appearance and the inner reality.

Banquo's honesty is a *foil* for Macbeth's deceit.

'Look like the innocent flower but be the serpent under't.'

'I dreamt last night of the three weird sisters'

The characters who are aligned with evil in the play deliberately lie and manipulate.

The characters aligned with good in the play are honest.

Appearance & Reality

Macbeth realises that he has been tricked by the witches.

Does the ending resolve the lies and deceit?

'juggling fiends'

Yes: With Malcolm as king, the audience is reassured that an open and honest rule is beginning.

Here, at his moment of *anagnorisis*, Macbeth realises that his faith in the witches has been misplaced and he has been deceived.

No: Deceit lies in all of us and Fleance, prophesised to be king one day, might be tempted to follow the same treacherous path of Macbeth.

Read the following extract from Act 1 Scene 5 of 'Macbeth'.
Answer both questions below the text.

At this point in the play, Macbeth has just returned home to Lady Macbeth.

MACBETH:
My dearest love,
Duncan comes here to-night.

LADY MACBETH:
And when goes hence?

MACBETH:
To-morrow, as he purposes.

LADY MACBETH:
O, never
Shall sun that morrow see!
Your face, my thane, is as a book where men
May read strange matters. To beguile the time,
Look like the time; bear welcome in your eye,
Your hand, your tongue: look like the innocent flower,
But be the serpent under't. He that's coming
Must be provided for: and you shall put
This night's great business into my dispatch.

a) How is the idea of appearance and reality presented in this extract?

b) How is the idea of appearance and reality presented in the play as a whole?

≡ Sample GCSE Answer

☑ **Start with an overview**

Lies and deceit lie at the heart of 'Macbeth'. In a world of **'fog and filthy air'**, it is not always easy to know who or what to trust, and Shakespeare explores this idea throughout the play. At this point in the play, Lady Macbeth instructs Macbeth in the art of deception.

☑ **Make the point that Lady Macbeth's language is dishonest**

The relationship between Lady Macbeth and Macbeth is a close one; Macbeth calls her **'my dearest love'**, an endearment that reflects the depth of love through the **superlative 'dearest'** and the **possessive pronoun 'my'**. Yet even in their loving relationship, there is a lack of honesty. Lady Macbeth's naked ambition and intention to commit murder is clearly stated in **'O, never shall sun that morrow see!'** This is honest, yet straight away she begins to use language of euphemisms (coded language). She refers to Duncan's cold-blooded murder as a **'great business'**. The language cloaks the reality of the action- that of killing a king. **'Great'** makes it sounds like an honourable and significant event while **'business'** suggests a necessary practicality which is backed up by the vague phrase **'he... must be provided for'**. The language itself is dishonest and it reflects a dishonesty between them. What they are planning to do is so dreadful that they have to hide the nasty reality from each other. This reflects the magnitude of the crime. In Jacobean times, kings were seen as chosen by God to rule and the killing of a king was therefore viewed as a crime against God that would disrupt the natural order of the world. No wonder the Macbeths cannot spell out what they are hoping to do in plain language.

☑ Make the point that Lady Macbeth is portrayed as less honest than Macbeth

Lady Macbeth urges Macbeth to be as deceitful as herself, saying **'look like the time; bear welcome in your eye/Your hand, your tongue'**. The *list* of body parts reflects how she wishes him to allow deception to consume him entirely and for him to deceive with all of his senses. She emphasises this by employing a *repetitive sentence structure* **'look like the innocent flower but be the serpent under't'**. Here the *enjambment* and the turning point of the word **'but'** highlight the deliberate slyness and the contrast between outward appearance and the inner reality. The *imagery* reminds the church-going Jacobean audience of the serpent in the Garden of Eden as Lady Macbeth's language links her to the weak woman who tempted Adam to disobey God. Shakespeare portrays her as deceitful and sinful, deliberately playing on contemporary perceptions of women as false and sly.

☑ Make the point that the witches deliberately confuse appearance and reality

Shakespeare uses other women in the play to establish his theme. The witches immediately create a sense of confusion in Act 1 with their chant **'fair is foul and foul is fair'**, showing us that things are not always as they seem. The use of *paradox* here highlights the power of the witches; they will give Macbeth **'fair'** prophecies yet these will end up with **'foul'** consequences. The *repetition* of the **'f'** sounds emphasises a sense of forceful power and the *monosyllabic* words enhance the sense of the chanting of a spell, perhaps a spell to blur the lines between what is real and what is imagined and therefore create chaos. Jacobean audiences, who firmly believed in the power of witches, would have been convinced by this and have been fearful of the malevolent evil that the witches will unleash.

☑ Move on to show how the theme of appearance/reality affects all characters

In Act 2, Banquo admits that **'I dreamt last night of the three weird sisters'**. Banquo's words show how he is still brooding on the predictions that his sons will be kings of Scotland. His open admission of how the witches have stayed on his mind is a direct *contrast* with Macbeth's lie **'I think not of them'**. The theme of appearance and reality is illustrated here through Banquo's open honest nature and Macbeth's deceit; Shakespeare uses him as a *foil* (contrast) to Macbeth. A twist to the theme of appearance and reality is evident when Macduff comes to join Malcolm in England and Malcolm tests Macduff's loyalty by pretending to be evil. Macduff passes the test and Malcolm's mind is now reassured as to Macduff's honourable intention, saying he has **'reconciled my thoughts/To thy good truth and honour'**. Malcolm proves himself as more cautious than his father, Duncan, who was too quick to put his **'absolute trust'** in others. The Jacobean audience lived in a world where betrayal and vying for power was common. They would approve of a king who proved to be shrewd and looked closely at whether their subjects were trustworthy.

☑ Move to the end of the play and explore whether the lies and deceits are resolved

Shakespeare used the classic five act play structure of the ancient Greeks which always ended with *resolution*. There is a sense of closure at the end of the play as the honest Malcolm promises in his statement that **'we will perform in measure, time and place'** an intention to rule in a balanced and clear way. His sense of integrity is highlighted by the reference to his position as rightful king, ruling **'by the grace of Grace'** which reinforces his position as a king chosen by God. The audience is reassured that Scotland is now on course for a more open, harmonious period. However, at the same time, the audience is uneasily aware that the prophecy of Banquo's children becoming kings has yet to come to pass. We wonder whether Fleance, Banquo's son, will also become motivated by powerful ambition and whether the peace in Scotland will last. The play starts and ends with the death of a traitor after civil war, and this cyclical *structure* reinforces this sense that Scotland is doomed to repeat the same pattern of treachery and lies as Shakespeare constantly explores human nature and how deceit lies in all of us.

11 Guilt

Exploration of a theme

Guilt is a theme that dominates the play and is illustrated through Macbeth's internal conflict and the constant blood imagery. Shakespeare focuses on the Macbeth's guilt to show that the crime of regicide (killing a king) was one that would haunt the criminals and lead them to destruction. The Jacobean audience, to whom the failed Gunpowder Plot was a very recent memory, would have appreciated this reminder.

'I see thee... I see thee still... with gouts of blood... there's no such thing'

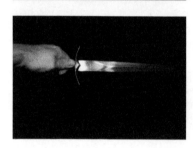

• Macbeth is experiencing a hallucination of a bloody dagger, guiding him towards the king's chamber. The hallucination represents his guilt; he knows that what he plans is terribly wrong.

• The *fragmented speech* shows Macbeth's unsettled mind as he contemplates the horror of his planned deed and is already extremely disturbed by his own actions. His internal conflict of ambition versus guilt is very clear.

• There is great *dramatic tension* as the audience wonders whether his guilt will prevent him from committing the crime.

Context: Shakespearean theatre would have been limited in terms of props and special effects so the hideous vocabulary of **'gouts of blood'** works hard to help the audience imagine the violent murder.

'I could not say 'Amen'

• Immediately after the regicide, Macbeth is consumed with guilt and is unable to say the traditional response to a religious blessing.

• His actions have placed him beyond God's love and comfort.

• *Structurally*, this is effective as it shows how quickly the guilt takes hold of Macbeth. The audience clearly sees how his ambition has taken him down a terrible path of mental torment.

Context: Regicide (killing of a king/queen) was seen as an appalling crime because it was a sin against God. The Jacobeans believed in the divine right of kings – that God anointed (chose) the monarch. The audience would understand the sacrilegious nature of Macbeth's crime and appreciate his overwhelming guilt.

'Sleep no more! Macbeth does murder sleep'	• Macbeth hears voices telling him that he will not sleep and that his conscience will be always tormented by his actions.
	• Sleep is a *motif* used to illustrate guilt throughout the play.
	• Macbeth murders Duncan while he is sleeping and therefore vulnerable. It is a cowardly act and one not worthy of the valiant brave soldier that Macbeth is meant to be. It is no wonder that he is consumed with guilt.
	• It *foreshadows* Lady Macbeth's sleepwalking which highlights her guilty conscience.

'Will all great Neptune's ocean wash this blood clean from my hand?' 	• Blood *imagery* is used to show guilt.
	• The *interrogative sentence* captures Macbeth's despair as he realises that the answer to his question is 'no' and that Duncan's blood will *metaphorically* stain him forever.
	• The *metaphor* reflects the enormity of his crime; not even the vastness of the ocean can clean him.
	• It *contrasts* with Lady Macbeth's pragmatic (practical) statement that **'a little water cleans us of this deed'**. Yet there is *dramatic irony* here; the audience remembers these dismissive words later on when she is obsessively washing her hands in Act 5 and see how untrue this is. In Act 5, her words echo Macbeth's

'Never shake thy gory locks at me!'	• Macbeth sees Banquo's ghost covered in gore and blood.
	• The ghost is a manifestation of the disorder in Macbeth's mind. Killing the King and Banquo has disturbed his mind's natural balance. Again, we see how consumed with guilt Macbeth is.
	• His language of blood shows the brutal violence of the murder. Macbeth's words emphasise to the audience how appalling the crime was, and so create tension and horror.

'Out, damned spot! out, I say!– One: two'

• Lady Macbeth is driven mad with guilt, trying to rub away imaginary blood.

• The *imperative verb* 'out' is *repeated* here to capture her desperation to rid herself of the bloodstain. It *contrasts* sharply with the use of *imperatives* in Act 1 when she turns to evil. Then she had power and control but here she has none; her guilty conscience has stripped her of any sense of power.

• The *fragmented speech* indicated by the *dashes* reflect her mental disorder as her natural balance is destroyed by her guilt. This is further shown through the use of *prose*, rather than blank verse, which again illustrates how guilt has sent her mad.

Grade 9 Exploration:
Look at the theme in a different way

Does Macbeth's guilt redeem him as a person?

Yes: Macbeth's guilt destroys his peace of mind and prevents him from enjoying his power. His clear sense of guilt is shown to the audience through the use of *soliloquies*, revealing his internal struggles. The audience also sees the dramatic visual manifestations of his guilt: the dagger and Banquo's ghost. By allowing us to so clearly witness Macbeth's guilt, Shakespeare creates a tragic hero whose bloody ambition is tempered (balanced) by his very human guilt.

No: Macbeth is fully aware of his guilt and culpability (responsibility) yet carries on with his murderous actions. This suggests a chilling lack of morality. We cannot sympathise with either him or Lady Macbeth; they have both knowingly commited a crime against family, hospitality, country and God. Their dreadful, destructive guilt is well-deserved.

Essential Exam Tips

☑ Be prepared for your exam. Learn the quotations in this guide and the analysis which goes with them.

☑ A good way to do this is to write quotations out onto sticky notes and place them on your bathroom mirror/kettle/fridge door- i.e. places that you go to all of the time! That way you keep seeing them and they will lodge themselves into your memory.

Regicide was seen as an appalling crime because it was a sin against God. Macbeth realises that he has put himself beyond God's love and comfort.

The *metaphor* reflects the enormity of Macbeth's crime; not even the vastness of the ocean can clean him.

'I could not say 'Amen''

'Will all great Neptune's ocean wash this blood clean from my hand?'

Guilt is a result of the enormity of the Macbeths' crime.

Blood *imagery* is used to show guilt.

Guilt

A sleep motif is used to illustrate guilt.

Does Macbeth's guilt redeem him?

'Sleep no more!'

Yes: Macbeth's guilt destroys his peace of mind and prevents him from enjoying his power and we pity him.

Macbeth knows that he will not sleep again; his conscience will be always tormented by his actions. His words *foreshadow* Lady Macbeth's guilty sleepwalking.

No: Macbeth is fully aware of his guilt yet carries on with his murderous actions. This suggests a chilling lack of morality.

Read the following extract from Act 2 Scene 2 of 'Macbeth'.
Answer both questions below the text.

At this point in the play, Macbeth has just killed King Duncan.

MACBETH:
Still it cried 'Sleep no more!' to all the house:
'Glamis hath murder'd sleep, and therefore Cawdor
Shall sleep no more; Macbeth shall sleep no more.'

LADY MACBETH:
Who was it that thus cried? Why, worthy thane,
You do unbend your noble strength, to think
So brainsickly of things. Go get some water,
And wash this filthy witness from your hand.
Why did you bring these daggers from the place?
They must lie there: go carry them; and smear
The sleepy grooms with blood.

MACBETH:
I'll go no more:
I am afraid to think what I have done;
Look on't again I dare not.

a) Discuss how the idea of guilt is presented in this extract.
b) Discuss how the idea of guilt is presented in the play as a whole.

 Sample GCSE Answer

☑ Start with an overview

Guilt is a theme that dominates the play and is illustrated through Macbeth's internal conflict and the constant blood ***imagery***. Shakespeare focuses on the Macbeth's guilt to show that the crime of regicide was one that would haunt the criminals and lead them to destruction. The Jacobean audience, to whom the failed Gunpowder Plot was a very recent memory, would have appreciated this reminder, and here in the extract, just after Macbeth has killed the king, the audience sees just how quickly the guilt of their crime consumes the Macbeths.

☑ Make the point that Macbeth is clearly overcome with guilt

Shakespeare uses a sleep ***motif*** which is revisited throughout the play to constantly emphasise the guilty consciences of the Macbeths. Macbeth murders Duncan while he is sleeping and therefore vulnerable; it is a cowardly act and one not worthy of the valiant brave soldier that Macbeth is meant to be. No wonder he is consumed with guilt. Immediately after killing Duncan, Macbeth hears voices, **'still it cried 'Sleep no more!'** The voices show his unbalanced mind, disturbed by the enormity of his crime of regicide. It is significant that the voices tell him that he will **'sleep no more'**; this is ***repeated*** for maximum impact, to reinforce how he has completely destroyed the peace of mind that sleep brings. The ***modal verb*** **'shall'** is used twice to demonstrate the certainty with which Macbeth knows that he has placed himself beyond morality and serenity. The voices ***foreshadow*** the sleepwalking of Lady Macbeth. Lady Macbeth emphatically denies the enormity of Duncan's murder yet her guilt is shown through her subconscious; when she sleepwalks at the end of the play, she admits her guilt in the bloodshed several times. From a psychological point of view, Lady Macbeth's suppressed guilt cannot be contained; it manifests itself in her sleepwalking.

☑ **Develop the point about the enormity of the crime leading to a huge sense of guilt**

The Jacobean audience would have understood the guilt, seeing the crime of regicide as an appalling one because it was a sin against God. The Jacobeans believed in the divine right of kings, that God anointed the monarch. This was part of the belief of the Great Chain of Being, that everyone in society had his/her place with the king at the top and that murdering a king disrupted the natural order. In this same scene, Macbeth is consumed with guilt and is unable to say the traditional response to a religious blessing, claiming that **'I could not say 'Amen'**. His actions have placed him beyond God's love and comfort and have left him with a crippling sense of guilt as he refuses to go back to the chamber, saying **'look on't again I dare not.'**

☑ **Link the above point to the ideas that guilt is linked to concepts of manhood**

Macbeth is overcome with anguish at his own crime but Lady Macbeth attempts to rally (encourage) him with **'why, worthy thane/you do unbend your noble strength, to think/So brainsickly of things'**. Feeling guilt and being strong are seen as incompatible (unable to exist together) by Lady Macbeth. Jacobean audiences viewed manhood in terms of being fearless and here Lady Macbeth sees Macbeth's guilt and fear of his own actions as something which weakens him. Yet Shakespeare is showing Lady Macbeth's version of manhood as simply being without morality which is not so much unmanly as inhumane. It is Macbeth's human guilt which saves him from being a monster.

☑ **Move on to show how the idea of guilt is shown using blood imagery**

Blood *imagery* is used to show guilt. In the extract, Lady Macbeth orders Macbeth to **'wash this filthy witness from your hand'**. However, the blood is a symbol of his guilt and cannot be cleansed. Macbeth knows this, later asking: **'will all great Neptune's ocean wash this blood/Clean from my hand?'** The *interrogative sentence* shows Macbeth's despair as he realises that the answer is no- that Duncan's blood will *metaphorically* stain him forever. The *metaphor* reflects the enormity of his crime- not even the vastness of the ocean can clean him. It *contrasts* with Lady Macbeth's pragmatic **'a little water cleans us of this deed'**. Yet there is *dramatic irony* here; the audience remembers these practical words later on when she is obsessively washing her hands in Act 5 and we see how untrue this is. In Act 5, her words echo Macbeth's ocean *metaphor* as she says **'all the perfumes of Arabia will not sweeten this little hand'**. The *image* of the heavy scents of the myriad perfumes of an exotic land shows how nothing can eradicate her guilt.

☑ **Move to the end of the play and explore whether Macbeth's guilt redeems him as a person**

Macbeth's guilt destroys his peace of mind and prevents him enjoying his power. His clear sense of guilt is revealed to the audience through the dramatic visual *images* of guilt and the use of *soliloquies* showing his internal struggles. By allowing us to so clearly witness Macbeth's guilt, Shakespeare creates a tragic hero whose bloody ambition is tempered (balanced) by his very human remorse; we cannot help but feel pity for him as his overwhelming guilt destroys him. Yet this sense of pity is not a given. Macbeth is fully aware of his guilt and culpability (responsibility) yet carries on with his murderous actions. This suggests a chilling lack of morality. For example, in Act 2, Macbeth experiences a hallucination of a bloody dagger, guiding him towards the king's chamber- **'I see thee... I see thee still... with gouts of blood... there's no such thing'**. The dagger is a visual representation of his guilt and useful in terms of staging as Shakespearean theatre would have been limited in terms of props and special effects so the vivid language works hard to help the audience imagine the dagger. The *fragmented speech* shows Macbeth's unsettled mind as he contemplates the horror of his planned deed, yet finally he deliberately puts his humanity and morals to one side and kills the king in cold blood. His terrible, destructive guilt for his crime that ruins his peace of mind and his kingship is fully deserved.

Shakespeare explores the concept of masculinity and femininity in 'Macbeth'. The idea of what qualities defined men and women in the Jacobean era weaves its way through the play.

'brave Macbeth'

• Macbeth is described with the **epithet 'brave'** as he fights for his king and country.

• Shakespeare establishes him as the epitome (best example) of a courageous, honourable man.

Context: The Jacobean era was one of political and social unrest. Military strength was seen as an important part of being a man.

'Come, you spirits that tend on mortal thoughts, unsex me here'

• Lady Macbeth rejects her female qualities of kindness and nurturing in order to gain power.

• She sees these feminine qualities as inhibiting (stopping) her from having the strength to commit murder.

• Her **imperative verbs 'come'** and **'unsex'** show her deliberate decision to abandon her natural womanhood and embrace evil.

Context: The Jacobean audience believed that women were natural nurturers, meek and subservient. Lady Macbeth's desire for power would have been very shocking to a Jacobean audience, who would have found it unnatural and disturbing.

'I dare do all that may become a man. Who dares do more is none'

• Macbeth understands that killing the king will completely change him as a person.

• He is brave and strong enough to do noble, heroic actions but killing the king is not the action of a brave man. The murder will unman him.

Context: In the Jacobean era, regicide was seen as an appalling crime because it was a sin against God. Part of the concept of being a man was loyalty to the king and to God.

'When you durst do it, then you were a man'	• Lady Macbeth uses ideas of manhood to manipulate her husband into killing Duncan. • She taunts him with a lack of courage, saying that a real man would kill the king.	**Context:** Women were seen as the weaker sex yet here Lady Macbeth takes control over her husband.

'give to the edge o' the sword/his wife, his babes'	• Macbeth's desire for complete power leads him to despicable acts such as the murder of Macduff's family. • The *imperative verb* shows his cold-hearted sense of purpose and the use of **'babes'**, *symbol* of innocence, illustrates that Macbeth is fully aware of what he is ordering. • Ambition has stripped Macbeth of all compassion; he is now more monster than man.

'but I must feel it like a man'	• Macduff is told of the murder of his wife and children and says that he must feel his grief **'like a man'**. • Shakespeare uses Macduff to demonstrate that being a man is not just about being physically fearless; being a man has many levels of complexity, and feeling emotions such as love and grief is part of being a true man. • Macduff's emotion acts as a **foil** to Macbeth's lack of emotion.

'all the perfumes of Arabia will not sweeten this little hand. Oh, oh, oh!' 	• Lady Macbeth's ambition sends her mad. Her *fragmented speech* and unstructured **'oh oh oh'** show her at the very end as weak and broken. • The crimes she has committed are so unnatural that she has been stripped of the 'masculine' qualities that allowed her to plan murder. She is broken by her part in the murder and any strength of character has been eaten away by the terrible guilt.

'But, bear-like, I must fight the course'

- Macbeth dies with honour and bravery.

- The *simile* of **'bear-like'** illustrates his determination to die bravely. Bears were seen as noble and the comparison shows that, despite his crimes, Macbeth still retains the vestiges (remains) of nobility.

- He does not die a coward's death and, at the end, he is **'brave Macbeth'** and the epitome of a fearless fighter.

Grade 9 Exploration:
Look at the theme in a different way

Does Shakespeare present a world where women are the most powerful sex?

Yes: The **'weird sisters'** drive the plot, controlling the characters and exploiting their weaknesses. Their chant in the opening scene of **'fair is foul and foul is fair'** establishes their power, with the *repetition* of the **'f'** sounds emphasising a sense of forceful strength and the *monosyllabic* words enhancing the sense of the chanting of a potent spell. Macbeth's first words link him to these witches as he says **'so fair and foul a day'**, immediately linking him with the forces of evil and suggesting that this brave, heroic man is already being manipulated by the strange, unearthly witches. Lady Macbeth is also incredibly powerful as she manipulates her husband and commands him to **'look like the innocent flower/ but be the serpent under't'**. The *enjambment* and the turning point of the word **'but'** highlights the deliberate slyness that Lady Macbeth employs to control and direct her husband.

No: The women have to take on masculine qualities in order to wield power; the **'weird sisters'** have beards and Lady Macbeth, a weak woman, has to be **'unsex(ed)'** to fulfil her desires. Furthermore, it is Malcolm who is firmly in control at the end (see context box below).

Shakespeare's original audience held a firm belief in a sense of order within society where men were naturally in control and women were subservient. The women in 'Macbeth' who seize power do so in clearly unnatural ways and only bring chaos, violence and bloodshed in their wake. The Jacobean audience would have been satisfied with the ascension of Macolm; as a strong male and the rightful heir, he brings a restoration of order and calm to the world which women have challenged.

Macbeth begins the play as the epitome of a man: loyal, physically brave and noble.

Lady Macbeth accuses Macbeth of lacking manly qualities so that he will agree to kill King Duncan.

'brave Macbeth'

'When you durst do it, then you were a man'

Manhood is seen in terms of strength.

Lady Macbeth uses ideas of manhood is used to manipulate Macbeth.

Masculine/Feminine

Macduff is used to illustrate true manhood.

Does Shakespeare show a world where women are the most powerful sex?

'but I must feel it like a man'

Yes: The **'weird sisters'** drive the plot and Lady Macbeth is also powerful, controlling her husband.

Being a man has many levels of complexity and feeling emotions such as love and grief is part of being a true man.

No: The women have to take on masculine qualities in order to wield power; the **'weird sisters'** have beards and Lady Macbeth is only powerful once 'unsex(ed)'.

Sample GCSE Exam Question

Read the following extract from Act 3 Scene 4 of 'Macbeth'. Answer both questions below the text.

At this point in the play, Macbeth has just seen the ghost of Banquo.

LADY MACBETH:
Are you a man?
MACBETH:
Ay, and a bold one, that dare look on that
Which might appal the devil.
LADY MACBETH:
O proper stuff!
This is the very painting of your fear:
This is the air-drawn dagger which, you said,
Led you to Duncan. O, these flaws and starts,
Impostors to true fear, would well become
A woman's story at a winter's fire,
Authorized by her grandam. Shame itself!
Why do you make such faces? When all's done,
You look but on a stool.
MACBETH:
Prithee, see there! behold! look! lo!
how say you?
Why, what care I? If thou canst nod, speak too.
If charnel-houses and our graves must send
Those that we bury back, our monuments
Shall be the maws of kites.

a) Discuss how ideas of gender are presented in this extract.
b) Discuss how ideas of gender are presented in the play as a whole.

Sample GCSE Answer

✓ **Start with an overview**

Shakespeare explores the concept of masculinity and femininity in 'Macbeth'. The idea of what qualities defined men and women in the Jacobean era weaves its way throughout the play and in the extract, we see Lady Macbeth and Macbeth struggling with their emotions in a volatile situation that challenges their views of how men and women should behave.

✓ **Make the point that Lady Macbeth constantly challenges Macbeth's masculinity**

In the extract, Lady Macbeth constantly erodes at Macbeth's masculinity and the use of the *interrogative sentence structure* **'are you a man?'** is a direct challenge, with the blunt *monosyllables* creating a sense of angry confrontation. It also reflects her anxiety; Macbeth is behaving very strangely in a public place and thereby is undermining his authority. The Jacobean audience, living in turbulent political times, valued strong male leadership and yet here Macbeth is starting and flinching at visions. She is using masculinity to try to manipulate Macbeth by eroding his sense of manhood; this is the same tactic that she employs in Act 1 when she taunts him to kill Duncan, saying **'when you durst do it, then you were a man.'** Women in Jacobean times were seen as the weaker sex yet, at the start of the play, Lady Macbeth takes control over her husband. Interestingly, this tactic of shaming him through a lack of manhood does not work in this feast scene. Lady Macbeth's hold over her husband has slipped and appeals to his manhood are fruitless.

✅ Make the point that fear is seen as incompatible with manhood

Macbeth's horror at the vision of Banquo's ghost is shown by his *vocabulary* 'death' 'charnel house' 'bury' and **'monuments'** which creates a *semantic field* of death and evil that chills the audience. The ghost is a visual manifestation of his guilt and dramatically very powerful for the audience, especially a superstitious Jacobean audience. Lady Macbeth tries to dismiss this vision as merely **'a woman's story at a winter's fire/ Authorized by her grandam'**, again trying to undermine his manhood by accusing him of behaving more like a woman than a man. Interestingly, Macbeth's behaviour is belittled twice by Lady Macbeth referring to a young woman telling a ghost story and also a grandmother listening to it. Lady Macbeth is insisting that his behaviour is more suited to a women in a domestic situation, not a king and soldier. Yet, in the midst of the tension and drama of this scene, there is humour for the audience in her pragmatic line **'you look but on a stool'** and, through the humour, Lady Macbeth is seen as the strong character here, dismissing fear as folly and cowardice.

✅ Explore how Lady Macbeth is portrayed as an unnatural woman

The presentation of Lady Macbeth as a strong female is evident in the extract with her dismissive **'o proper stuff!'**, the *exclamatory sentence* reflecting her contempt for her husband. Yet this strength was not a quality expected or desired in a woman in Jacobean times. Lady Macbeth's disrespect would have been disapproved of by Jacobean audiences as unnatural feminine behaviour and, indeed, we have seen Lady Macbeth's unusual behaviour in Act 1 where she rejects her female qualities of nurturing in order to gain power. She turns to the forces of evil when she commands **'come you spirits that tend on mortal thoughts, unsex me here'**. She sees these feminine qualities as inhibiting her from having the strength to commit murder and her *imperative verbs* 'come' 'unsex' reflect her very deliberate decision to abandon her natural womanhood and embrace evil.

✅ Discuss how Shakespeare uses the character of Macduff to show manhood

Male emotions are also explored later in Act 4 when Macduff is told of the murder of his wife and children and says that he must feel his grief **'like a man'.** Shakespeare uses Macduff to show that being a man is not just about being physically fearless; being a man has many levels of complexity and feeling emotions such as love and grief is part of being a true man. Macduff's deep emotion acts as a *foil* to Macbeth's lack of emotion. Macbeth's desire for complete power leads him to despicable acts such as the murder of Macduff's family when he instructs his soldiers to **'give to the edge o' the sword/his wife, his babes'.** The *imperative verb* **'give'** reflects his cold-hearted sense of purpose and the use of the *noun* **'babes'**, *symbol* of innocence, illustrates that Macbeth is fully aware of what he is ordering. Ambition has made him more monster than man.

✅ Explore whether women are the most powerful sex

It would seem that women are the most powerful sex in the play as the **'weird sisters'** drive the plot, controlling the characters and exploiting their weaknesses. Their chant in the opening scene of **'fair is foul and foul is fair'** establishes their power; the *repetition* of the **'f'** sounds emphasises their forceful strength and the *monosyllabic* words enhance the sense of the chanting of a potent spell. Macbeth's first words link him to these witches as he says **'so fair and foul a day'**, immediately associating him with the forces of evil and suggesting that this brave, heroic man is already being manipulated by the strange, unearthly witches. Lady Macbeth is also incredibly powerful as she manipulates her husband, commanding him to **'look like the innocent flower/ but be the serpent under't'**. The *enjambment* and the turning point of the word **'but'** highlights the deliberate slyness that Lady Macbeth employs to control and direct her husband. Yet we should remember that these forceful women have to take on masculine qualities in order to wield power; the **'weird sisters'** have beards and Lady Macbeth, a weak woman, has to be **'unsex(ed)'** to fulfil her desires. Furthermore, it is Malcolm who is in control at the end, pleasing Shakespeare's original audience who held a firm belief in a sense of order within society where men were naturally in control and women were subservient. The women in 'Macbeth' who seize power do so in unnatural ways and only bring chaos and bloodshed in their wake. The Jacobean audience would have been satisfied with the ascension of Malcolm; as a strong male and the righful heir, he brings a restoration of order and calm to the world which women have challenged.

'Macbeth' is a play carefully constructed to have an enormous dramatic impact on the audience. Shakespeare uses many techniques to create drama and tension and seven of these are examined in this chapter: setting, dramatic irony, language, stage directions, dialogue, foreshadowing and juxtaposition.

'A desolate place: thunder and lightning. Enter three witches'

• The opening **setting** establishes an eerie atmosphere which immediately highlights the ominous (dangerous) presence of the witches and makes the audience uncomfortable and tense.

• The thunder and lightning shows a disturbance in nature. The **pathetic fallacy** warns the audience that a troubled time is coming.

• **Structurally,** Shakespeare opens the play with the **'three witches'**, emphasising their vital role.

Context: The Jacobean audience believed that disruption in nature (the macrocosm) reflected the human world (microcosm); Shakespeare uses the disturbance in nature to symbolise the potential disruption in the world of men. This would have created a sense of unease, compounded by the presence of the witches. The Jacobean audience firmly believed in their existence and malevolent (evil) power; King James 1 was so convinced that he wrote his own book, Daemonologie, on the subject. There is nothing comical or childish about these witches and Shakespeare's audience would have been chilled by their sinister presence.

'Hail to thee, Glamis/Cawdor/ King hereafter'

• **Dramatic irony** here builds the tension as the witches give their predictions.

• The audience knows that Duncan has already condemned the Thane of Cawdor and given his title to Macbeth, but Macbeth does not.

• We, the audience, know that the witches' predictions will come true. We wonder what Macbeth's reactions will be and anticipate his next move.

'I see thee... I see thee still... with gouts of blood... there's no such thing'

- *Language* works to create tension.

- The *structure* of the lines suggests that Macbeth's thoughts are unsettled, as even at this point he is unsure as to whether he will commit the crime of murder. This increases our tension as we watch and wonder but by the end of the *soliloquy* he has made up his mind and turns to Duncan's chamber.

Context: Shakespearean theatre would have been limited in terms of props and special effects so the hideous vocabulary of **'gouts of blood'** helps the audience imagine the scene.

An owl shrieks 'Hark, peace!'

- *Stage directions* create tension. Shakespeare holds us at the edge of our seats as we wait with Lady Macbeth for the news of the murder, unsure what will happen next.

- The sudden *sound effect* of the owl's cry makes Lady Macbeth, and us, jump. It could also *symbolise* nature protesting at the unnatural murder of an anointed king.

Context: Regicide (killing of a king) was seen as an appalling crime because it was a sin against God and disrupted the natural order. The murder of the king is off-stage to avoid showing a sacrilegious act.

'Did you not speak?/ When?/ Now?'

- *Dialogue* creates dramatic tension as Macbeth and Lady Macbeth worry that someone has caught them in the act of murdering the king. The short terse *interrogative sentences* between Lady Macbeth and Macbeth in this scene illustrate their barely contained panic.

- The questions show the desperate desire for information, the need to know that they are safe; their fear is conveyed through the *dialogue* and infects the audience.

'it will make us mad'

- *Foreshadowing* creates tension as Lady Macbeth tells Macbeth not to think back on the crime as it will send them both mad.

- The certainty of the *modal verb* **'will'** lays the way for the madness that comes later.

- *Structurally*, Shakespeare is preparing us for later events in the play, allowing us to predict what will happen, adding to the tension.

'devil/hell/ everlasting bonfire'

- *Juxtaposition* creates dramatic tension.

- The Porter is used to provide *comic relief*. Shakespeare deliberately uses him as a device to give the audience a respite (rest) from the high drama of the previous scene where Macbeth has just killed the king.

- His *prose* is comic and drunken which would amuse an audience but even here his language is dark, referencing the underworld of death and hell.

- The pause in the fast-moving action only increases our suspense as we wait for the body of Duncan to be discovered.

Grade 9 Exploration:
Explore how structure adds to the tension

Examine 'Macbeth' in the light of Greek tragedy

Shakespeare uses the structure of Greek tragedy to construct his play. This structure allows the audience to experience a range of emotions and for the pace and the tension to be maintained. Shakespeare creates a hero who has a fatal flaw or *hamartia*. In Macbeth's case, this fatal flaw is ambition. Although this fatal flaw changes him from honourable man to violent murderer, we still see human qualities and this makes us constantly and uneasily question ourselves as to how far we would go for power. The *exposition* of the play creates great conflict between Macbeth and society, and also conflict within himself, and then we follow the play's action with its violence and horror right up to Macbeth's moment of *anagnorisis*, when Macbeth realises that he has been tricked by the witches. There is *resolution* and *catharsis* at the end when Malcolm restores order to Scotland, allowing the audience a chance to reflect on the lessons of the play, released from the dramatic tension that has captured them for the last two hours.

Essential Exam Tips

☑ Use formal language throughout your response.

☑ Some of the exam boards will assess your spelling, punctuation and grammar on this question. Even if these skills are not assessed, you do need to write as well as you can.

The **setting** establishes an eerie atmosphere which highlights the dangerous presence of the witches and makes the audience uncomfortable and tense.

The audience knows that the witches' predictions will come true. We wonder what Macbeth's reactions will be and eagerly anticipate his next move.

'A desolate place:
thunder and lightning.
Enter three witches'

'Hail to thee, Glamis/
Cawdor/
King hereafter'

Tension is created through **setting**.

Tension is created through **dramatic irony**.

Drama & Tension

Language creates dramatic tension as Macbeth wonders whether to kill Duncan.

Stage directions create tension.

'I see thee... I see thee still... with gouts of blood...'

An owl shrieks 'Hark, peace!'

The **structure** of the lines suggests that Macbeth's thoughts are scattered. This increases our tension as we watch and wonder what he will do.

The **sound effect** of the owl's cry makes Lady Macbeth, and us, jump. It could also **symbolise** nature protesting at the unnatural murder of a king.

Read the following extract from Act 2 Scene 3 of 'Macbeth'.
Answer both questions below the text.

At this point in the play, Macduff has gone to wake the dead king.

LENNOX:
The night has been unruly: where we lay,
Our chimneys were blown down; and, as they say,
Lamentings heard i' the air; strange screams of death,
And prophesying with accents terrible
Of dire combustion and confused events
New hatch'd to the woeful time: the obscure bird
Clamour'd the livelong night: some say, the earth
Was feverous and did shake.

MACBETH:
'Twas a rough night.

LENNOX:
My young remembrance cannot parallel
A fellow to it.
Re-enter MACDUFF

MACDUFF:
O horror, horror, horror! Tongue nor heart
Cannot conceive nor name thee!

MACBETH / LENNOX:
What's the matter?

MACDUFF:
Confusion now hath made his masterpiece!
Most sacrilegious murder hath broke ope
The Lord's anointed temple, and stole thence
The life o' the building!

a) How is dramatic tension created in this extract?
b) How is dramatic tension created in the play as a whole?

 # Sample GCSE Answer

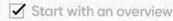 **Start with an overview**

'Macbeth' is a play carefully constructed to have an enormous dramatic impact on the audience. At this point in the play, the tension is almost palpable as Macduff exits the stage to wake the king. Only Macbeth, and the audience, know that the king will not wake because he is dead; our knowledge of the regicide allows us to experience the suspense and drama of the scene.

Make the point that a sense of tension is built through Ross' words

Lennox's words create a sense of great unease amongst the audience. The **semantic field** of chaos and disaster with **'unruly' 'blown down' 'confused events'** tells us that the night was wild indeed. The Jacobean audience believed that disruption in nature (the macrocosm) reflected the human world (microcosm); Shakespeare uses the disturbance in nature to symbolise the potential disruption in the world of men. This would have created a sense of disquiet for the audience. Another purpose for Lennox's long **description** is that it paints a picture for the audience. Shakespeare's theatre was very limited in terms of props and special effects so vivid **vocabulary** works hard here to help add to the drama of the wildness of the night. There is **humour** as Macbeth's **short sentence** 'twas a rough night' contrasts with Lennox's long speech, summarising the events of the night. This humour could work to **juxtapose** with the high tension of this scene and to provide much needed **comic relief**. Yet this is dark humour; Macbeth's night of murdering an old man in his bed was indeed a **'rough night'**.

✔ Move to the point that stage directions create tension

The tension is maintained through **dramatic irony**; the audience understands that Macbeth's version of the **'rough night'** is different to what Lennox assumes. **Dramatic irony** is used elsewhere as the witches give their predictions in Act 1 with **'hail to thee, Glamis, Cawdor, King'**. The audience knows that Duncan has condemned Cawdor and given the title to Macbeth, but Macbeth does not. We, the audience, know that the witches' predictions will come true and we wonder what Macbeth's reactions will be, anticipating his next move. In the extract, a further purpose of Lennox's speech is that it allows time for Macduff to find the body of the king. We anticipate this discovery and so the **stage direction 're-enter Macduff'** works at ramping up the tension to intense levels. Again, Shakespeare uses **stage directions** elsewhere to create tension, for example in Act 2 when we wait with Lady Macbeth for the news of the murder, unsure what will happen next. The **sound effect** of **'an owl shrieks'** makes Lady Macbeth, and us, jump. The owl's cry could also **symbolise** nature protesting at the unnatural murder of an anointed king, and this horrific concept of regicide puts the audience on edge.

✔ Link the above point to the idea that the concepts explored create tension

Dialogue is used to add drama to the scene as Macduff cries **'horror horror horror'**. The **repetition** emphasises the hideousness of the sight that he has just seen and shows that it so awful that he cannot find words. Again, this increases tension as information is withheld from Lennox. Macduff then expresses his complete outrage at seeing Duncan's dead body by **personifying** murder as a thief, saying **'most sacrilegious murder hath broke ope/The Lord's anointed temple'**. The **religious imagery** reflects the magnitude of the crime. Duncan is seen as an anointed temple, someone sacred and untouchable. The **plosive** sound of **'broke'** captures the violence of the crime against someone so pure, and reminds the audience, for whom Guy Fawkes' Gunpowder Plot was a very recent memory, of the dreadfulness of the crime. This would add to the drama and tension of this pivotal scene.

✔ Move to other parts of the play to show how *dramatic tension* is created

Dialogue is used elsewhere to create tension; earlier in Act 2, Macbeth and Lady Macbeth worry that someone has caught them in the act of murdering the king, saying **'did you not speak?/When?/Now?'** Their short terse **interrogative sentences** illustrate their barely contained panic, their desperate desire for information, the need to know that they are safe; their fear is conveyed through the **dialogue** and infects the audience. **Foreshadowing** is another device used; Lady Macbeth tells Macbeth not to think back on the crime as **'it will make us mad'**. The certainty of the **modal verb 'will'** lays the way for the madness that comes later. **Structurally**, Shakespeare is preparing us for later events in the play, allowing us to become invested in the play and to predict what will happen, adding to the tension.

✔ Examine dramatic tension in the light of Greek tragedy

Shakespeare uses the structure of Greek tragedy to construct his play, a structure which allows the audience to experience a range of emotions and for the pace and tension to be maintained. Shakespeare creates a hero who has a fatal flaw or **hamartia**. In Macbeth's case, this fatal flaw is ambition. Although this fatal flaw changes him from honourable man to violent murderer, we still see human qualities and this makes us constantly and uneasily question ourselves as to how far we would go for power. The **exposition** of the play creates great conflict between Macbeth and society and also within himself, and then we follow the play's action with its violence and horror right up to Macbeth's moment of **anagnorisis**, when Macbeth realises that he has been tricked by the witches. There is **resolution** and **catharsis** at the end when Malcolm restores order to Scotland, allowing the audience a chance to reflect on the lessons of the play, released from the dramatic tension that has captured them for the last two hours.

The idea of conflict and disruption is embedded in the play as Shakespeare creates a world where the natural order is subverted with dreadful consequences.

'thunder and lightning'

- The opening of the play immediately establishes the idea of a disturbance in nature.

- Shakespeare deliberately uses **pathetic fallacy** to establish a dangerous, unsettled atmosphere which troubles the audience and creates tension from the beginning.

Context: The Jacobean audience believed that disruption in nature (the macrocosm) reflected the human world (microcosm). Shakespeare uses the disturbance in nature to symbolise the potential disruption in the world of men.

'fair is foul and foul is fair'

- The witches create a sense of confusion and disorder, showing us that things are not always as they seem. Their agenda is to wreak havoc on the world of men.

- The use of **paradox** here highlights the power of the witches; they will give him **'fair'** prophecies yet these will end up with **'foul'** consequences. The **repetition** of the 'f' sounds emphasises a sense of forceful power and the **monosyllabic** words enhance the sense of the chanting of a spell. They show their power in brewing mischief and disorder.

- Shakespeare establishes an atmosphere of malevolent power right at the beginning, establishing a world where nothing is as it seems and is therefore dangerous.

Context: The Jacobean audience believed in the existence of witches with their malevolent power; King James 1 was so convinced that he wrote his own book, Daemonologie, on the subject. Shakespeare's audience would have been chilled by their evil presence, firmly believing in their power to disrupt.

'Come, you spirits that tend on mortal thoughts, unsex me here'

- Lady Macbeth subverts the natural order by rejecting her womanhood.

- Her *imperative verbs* reflect her deliberate decision to abandon her natural womanhood and embrace evil, thereby choosing disorder.

Context: The Jacobean audience believed that women were natural nurturers, meek and subservient. Lady Macbeth's actions would have been very shocking to a Jacobean audience who would find this **soliloquy** startling and unnatural.

'Most sacrilegious murder hath broke ope/The Lord's anointed temple, and stole thence the life o' the building!'

- Macduff expresses his complete horror at seeing Duncan's dead body by *personifying* murder as a thief.

- The *religious imagery* reflects the magnitude of the crime. Duncan is seen as an anointed temple, someone sacred and untouchable. The *plosive* sound of **'broke'** shows the violence of the crime against someone so pure.

- There are many references to the disruption in nature that this murder has caused; Lennox states that the **'night has been unruly'** and **'the earth did shake'** which reflects how nature has been disturbed by the dreadful, sacriligious crime of killing Duncan.

Context: Regicide (killing of a king/queen) was seen as an appalling crime because it was a sin against God. The Jacobeans believed in the divine right of kings, that God anointed (chose) the monarch. This was part of the belief in the Great Chain of Being, that everyone in society had his/her place with the king at the top. Murdering a king disrupted the natural order.

'Never shake thy gory locks at me!'

- Macbeth sees Banquo's ghost covered in gore and blood.

- The ghost is a manifestation of the disorder in Macbeth's mind. Killing the King and Banquo has disturbed his mind's natural balance. Again, we see how consumed with guilt Macbeth is; this guilt has unsettled his mind.

- The language of **'gory'** blood captures the horrific violence of the murder. Macbeth's words emphasise to the audience how horrific the crime was and so create tension and horror.

> **'Out, damned spot! out, I say!– One: two'**

- Lady Macbeth is driven mad with guilt, trying to rub away imaginary blood.

- **The imperative verb** 'out' is **repeated** here to reflect her desperation to rid herself of the bloodstain. It **contrasts** sharply with the use of **imperatives** in Act 1 when she turns to evil. Then she had power and control but here she has none; disorder is paramount.

- The **fragmented speech**, indicated by the **dashes**, illustrates her mental disorder as her natural balance is destroyed by her guilt. This is also shown through the use of **prose** rather than the **blank verse** she previously used.

Grade 9 Exploration:
Look at the theme in a different way

Is order restored at the end of the play?

Yes: Shakespeare uses the character of Malcolm to show the restoration of order at the end. Malcolm is Duncan's rightful heir so takes his place as King of Scotland, saying **'by the grace of Grace/We will perform in measure, time and place'**. Shakespeare used the classic five act play **structure** of the ancient Greeks which always ended with **resolution** and there is a sense of closure at the end of the play with the audience being reassured that lessons will be learned from the tragedy. The **rhyming couplets** in this final speech help give the play this sense of **resolution** and conclusion and the reference to God indicates that the Great Chain of Being is re-established. The use of the **triplet** **'measure, time and place'** creates a sense of controlled rhythm which gives the audience confidence that King Malcolm will bring peace and order to Scotland. This was important to the Jacobean audience to whom the anxiety over who would succeed the throne after Elizabeth died was still a very recent memory.

No: The audience is uneasily aware that the prophecy of Banquo's children becoming kings has yet to come to pass. We wonder whether Fleance, Banquo's son, will also become motivated by powerful ambition which destroys peace and the natural order. The play starts and ends with the death of a traitor after civil war, and this cyclical **structure** reinforces this sense that Scotland is doomed to repeat the same pattern, and that disorder will soon return to ravage Scotland again.

Essential Exam Tips

☑ Now you're at the end of this guide, you can see how easy it is to 'recycle' the same ideas. This should help you revise efficiently and effectively.

Disrupted weather was thought to reflect disruption in the world of men. This creates an uneasy sense of disorder from the beginning.

The use of **paradox** here highlights the power of the witches to disrupt. The **alliteration** also emphasises their power.

'thunder and lightning'

'fair is foul and foul is fair'

There is disturbance in nature.

The witches are seen as deliberately causing chaos.

Order & Disorder

There is mental disorder.

Is order restored at the end of the play?

'Out, damned spot! out, I say!--One: two'

Yes: With Malcolm as king, the audience is reassured that order is restored in Scotland.

Lady Macbeth's **fragmented speech** in **prose** shows how her mind is now disordered and broken through guilt.

No: The audience is uneasily aware that the prophecy that Fleance will become king has yet to pass, and that bloodshed and disorder might yet again rock Scotland.

Sample GCSE Exam Question

Read the following extract from Act 3 Scene 4 of 'Macbeth'.
Answer both questions below the text.

At this point in the play, Macbeth's feast to celebrate his coronation has been disrupted by Macbeth's visions of the ghost of Banquo.

LADY MACBETH:
You have displaced the mirth, broke the good meeting,
With most admired disorder.

MACBETH:
Can such things be,
And overcome us like a summer's cloud,
Without our special wonder? You make me strange
Even to the disposition that I owe,
When now I think you can behold such sights,
And keep the natural ruby of your cheeks,
When mine is blanched with fear.

ROSS:
What sights, my lord?

LADY MACBETH:
I pray you, speak not; he grows worse and worse;
Question enrages him. At once, good night:
Stand not upon the order of your going,
But go at once.

a) Write about how the idea of disorder is presented in this extract.
b) Write about how the idea of disorder is presented in the play.

Sample GCSE Answer

 Start with an overview

The idea of conflict and disruption is embedded in the play as Shakespeare creates a world where the natural order is subverted with dreadful consequences. In the extract, this disruption is dramatically evident as Macbeth's feast disintegrates into chaos.

☑ Macbeth's behaviour has caused the feast to disintegrate into chaos

Lady Macbeth's tone is bitter as she remonstrates Macbeth for disrupting the feast, saying **'you have displaced the mirth, broke the good meeting/With most admired disorder.'** The *tone* of **'admired disorder'** is sarcastic; this feast was a chance to consolidate Macbeth's position as king yet he has been hysterically shouting at visions. There is a sharp *contrast* from the start of the scene when Macbeth tells his guests to sit down in order of rank and the end of the scene when Lady Macbeth tells the guests to **'stand not upon the order of your going/But go at once'**. The *repetition* of **'at once'** shows the urgency with which she speaks as do the two *imperative verbs* **'stand' 'go'** in quick succession. The feast now has no gravtias or order; it is not a symbol of Macbeth's authority. Instead, it is a fiasco to be ended as soon as possible.

Make the point that Macbeth's mind is being disrupted through guilt

Macbeth is in horror at how his vision means that, while the thanes **'keep the natural ruby of (their) cheeks'**, his own cheeks are **'blanched with fear'**. The use of colour contrast here, white with red, reflects the unnatural state of his whole being as he is transfixed with horror at Banquo's ghost. The use of *interrogative sentence structures* further reflect a sense of confusion and lack of order as Macbeth asks **'can such things be..?'** Macbeth's uncertainty and disorder is infectious as Ross picks up with his own question, **'what sights, my lord?'** The men's doubt and apprehension create a real sense of unease, of an uncertainty about the world. The visions at the feast reflect the mental disorder of Macbeth's mind, just as the dagger did in Act 1 and Macbeth's hearing of voices calling **'sleep no more'** in Act 2. The mental disruption illustrates Macbeth's overwhelming sense of guilt at his crimes, and also reflect how his actions have plunged society into chaos. The Jacobean audience would have understood the guilt as the crime of regicide was an appalling one because it was a sin against God. They believed in the divine right of kings which formed part of the belief of the Great Chain of Being, that everyone in society had his/her place with the king at the top. Murdering a king disrupted this natural order. Later in Act 2, Macduff expresses his complete horror at seeing Duncan's dead body by *personifying* murder as a thief- **'most sacrilegious murder hath broke ope/The Lord's anointed temple, and stole thence the life o' the building!'** The religious *imagery* reflects the magnitude of the crime as Duncan is seen as an anointed temple, someone sacred and untouchable. There are many references to the disruption in nature that this murder has caused; Lennox states that the **'night has been unruly'** and **'the earth did shake'** which illustrates how nature has been disturbed by the sacrilegious crime of regicide.

 Move to another part of the play to show how the witches create disorder

Shakespeare establishes an atmosphere of malevolent power right at the beginning, establishing a world where nothing is ordered or as it seems and is therefore dangerous. The witches are associated with disorder as they enter to **'thunder and lightning'**. This *pathetic fallacy* creates a sense of unease as it connects them with disruption of nature; the Jacobean audience believed that disruption in nature (the macrocosm) reflected the human world (microcosm). The witches create a sense of confusion from the beginning with **'fair is foul and foul is fair'**, showing us that things are not always as they seem. Their agenda is to wreak havoc on the world of men, and the use of *paradox* here highlights the power of the witches; they will give Macbeth **'fair'** prophecies yet these will end up with **'foul'** consequences. The *repetition* of the **'f'** sounds emphasises a sense of forceful power and the *monosyllabic* words enhance the sense of the chanting of a spell as they brew disorder. The Jacobean audience believed in the existence of witches with their malevolent power; King James 1 was so convinced that he wrote a book, Daemonologie, on the subject. Shakespeare's audience would have been chilled by their presence and would have believed in their power to disrupt the natural order.

 Explore how Shakespeare shows that order is restored at the end of the play

Shakespeare uses the character of Malcolm to show the restoration of order at the end. Malcolm is Duncan's rightful heir so takes his place as King of Scotland, saying **'by the grace of Grace/We will perform in measure, time and place'**. Shakespeare used the classic five act play *structure* of the ancient Greeks which always ended with *resolution*, and there is a sense of closure at the end of the play with the audience being reassured that lessons will be learned from the tragedy. The *rhyming couplets* in this final speech help give the play this sense of *resolution*, and the reference to God shows that the Great Chain of Being is re-established. The use of the *triplet* **'measure, time and place'** creates a sense of controlled rhythm which gives the audience confidence that King Malcolm will bring peace to Scotland. This was important to the Jacobean audience for whom the anxiety over who would succeed the throne after Elizabeth died was still a recent memory. However, this reassurance that order is established is undermined, perhaps, by the knowledge that that the prophecy of Banquo's children becoming kings has yet to come to pass. We wonder whether Fleance will also become motivated by powerful ambition which destroys peace and the natural order. The play starts and ends with the death of a traitor after civil war, and this cyclical *structure* reinforces this sense that Scotland is doomed to repeat the same pattern, and that disorder will soon return to ravage Scotland again.

Quotations

Recap & Revise

Act 1 Scene 1

'A desolate place: thunder and lightning. Enter three witches'
The opening setting establishes a sinister atmosphere.

'Fair is foul and foul is fair'
The witches create a sense of confusion.

'As sparrows eagles, or the hare the lion'
Macbeth and Banquo are described as incredibly brave.

'Go pronounce his present death/And with his former title greet Macbeth'
King Duncan gives the title of Thane of Cawdor to Macbeth.

Act 1 Scene 2

'Brave Macbeth'
Macbeth is described as a courageous soldier.

Act 1 Scene 3

'So foul and fair a day'
Macbeth's opening words comment on the day and weather and associate him with the witches.

'Thrice'
The witches complete their spell by repeating the word 'thrice' (three).

'Hail to thee, Glamis/Cawdor/King hereafter'
The witches give Macbeth their prophecies.

'Lesser than Macbeth, and greater'
The witches give Banquo a deliberately confusing prophecy.

'Chance may crown me without my stir'
Macbeth decides to let Fate control events.

Act 1 Scene 4

'He was a gentleman on whom I built/An absolute trust'
Duncan talks about how he completely trusted the traitor Cawdor.

'I have begun to plant thee'
Duncan tells Macbeth how he will nurture and support him.

'There if I grow, the harvest is your own'
Banquo responds humbly to Duncan's love and praise, pledging his loyalty.

'Stars, hide your fires; let not light see my black and deep desires'
Macbeth knows that he must keep his evil ambition secret.

Act 1 Scene 5

'Dearest partner in greatness'
Macbeth addresses Lady Macbeth with affection in his letter.

'Come, you spirits...come'
Lady Macbeth turns to the forces of evil and

welcomes the dark spirits who will strip her of her femininity.

'Look like the innocent flower/But be the serpent under't'
Lady Macbeth encourages Macbeth to deceive.

Act 1 Scene 7

'So meek... that his virtues will plead like angels, trumpet-tongued'
Duncan is described as a good man and great king.

I have no spur...but only vaulting ambition...which o'er leaps itself'
Macbeth is fully aware that his ambition is his only motivation in killing the king.

'When you durst do it, then you were a man'
Lady Macbeth manipulates Macbeth.

'I dare do all that may become a man. Who dares do more is none'
Macbeth tries to resist his wife's manipulation.

'plucked my nipple... dash'd the brains'
Lady Macbeth says she would rather kill her baby than act as Macbeth does.

Act 2 Scene 1

'I dreamt last night of the three weird sisters'
Banquo admits to thinking of the witches.

'Keep my allegiance clear'
Banquo is loyal to Duncan.

'I see thee... I see thee still... with gouts of blood... there's no such thing'
Macbeth experiences a hallucination of a bloody dagger.

Act 2 Scene 2

An owl shrieks 'Hark, peace!'
The stage direction and Lady Macbeth's response create a tense atmosphere.

'Had he not resembled my father as he slept, I had done it. My husband?'
Lady Macbeth waits for news of Duncan's murder, reflecting on how she was unable to kill him herself.

'Did you not speak?/When?/Now?'
Macbeth and Lady Macbeth show their tension.

'I could not say 'Amen''
Immediately after the regicide, Macbeth is consumed with guilt and is unable to say the response to a prayer.

'Sleep no more! Macbeth does murder sleep'
Macbeth hears voices telling him that he will not sleep; his conscience will always be tormented by his actions.

'It will make us mad'
Lady Macbeth warns Macbeth not to think back on their crime.

'Go get some water and wash this filthy witness from your hand'
Lady Macbeth orders her husband to wash the blood off his hands.

'Will all great Neptune's ocean wash this blood/Clean from my hand?'
Macbeth knows that his crime of regicide is unforgivable.

Act 2 Scene 3

'devil/hell/everlasting bonfire'
The Porter's jokes are full of dark references to hell.

'Most sacrilegious murder hath broke ope/the Lord's anointed temple, and stole thence the life o'the building'
Macduff expresses his complete horror at seeing Duncan's dead body.

'silver skin laced with his golden blood'
Macbeth describes how precious Duncan is.

'This murderous shaft that's shot hath not yet lighted'
When his father is murdered, Malcolm takes immediate action and flees to England.

Act 3 Scene 1

'play'dst most foully'
Banquo suspects Macbeth of killing Duncan.

'Come Fate into the list...champion me'
Macbeth is determined to hold onto the crown and defy the witches' prophecies.

Act 3 Scene 2

'my mind is full of scorpions'
Macbeth finds that becoming king does not bring him happiness.

'Be innocent of the knowledge, dearest chuck'
Macbeth confides less and less in his wife.

Act 3 Scene 4

'Enter the ghost of Banquo and sits in Macbeth's place'
Even though he has been murdered, Banquo is still a threat to Macbeth.

'Never shake thy gory locks at me!'
Macbeth flinches from Banquo's ghost's hair which is soaked in blood.

'Are you a man?'
Lady Macbeth tries to calm Macbeth by appealing to his manhood.

Act 4 Scene 1

'All this is so'
The witches state that their apparitions are true predictions.

'Give to the edge o' the sword/his wife, his babes'
Macbeth gives clear instructions to slaughter Macduff's wife and children.

Act 4 Scene 3

'Reconciled my thoughts/To thy good truth and honour'
Malcolm tests Macduff's loyalty.

'Give sorrow words'
Malcolm urges Macduff to speak about his grief.

'Dispute it like a man'
Malcolm tells Macduff to revenge himself on Macbeth.

'But I must feel it like a man'
Macduff acknowledges his grief at the murder of his wife and children.

Act 5 Scene 1

'Out damned spot! Out, I say!- One: two'

In her madness, Lady Macbeth sees visions of blood.

'All the perfumes of Arabia will not sweeten this little hand. O, O, O'
Lady Macbeth acknowledges in her madness the extent of her guilt.

'I would not have such a heart in my bosom'
The serving woman pities Lady Macbeth.

Act 5 Scene 4

'Let every soldier hew him down a branch'
Malcolm tells the soldiers to camoflage themselves with the trees from Birnham Wood.

Act 5 Scene 5

'She should have died hereafter'
Macbeth dismisses his wife's death in one sentence.

'Life's but a walking shadow, a poor player'
Macbeth reflects on the futility (pointlessness) of life.

Act 5 Scene 7

'But, bear-like, I must fight the course'
Macbeth dies with honour and courage.

Act 5 Scene 8

'juggling fiends'
Macbeth condemns the witches when he realises that they have tricked him.

'dead butcher' 'fiend-like queen'
Macduff condemns Macbeth and Lady Macbeth.

'By the grace of Grace/We will perform in measure, time and place'
Malcolm's words conclude the play, promising a kingship guided by wisdom and by God.

Act 5 Scene 9

'which would be planted newly'
Malcolm promises to rule in a positive way.

Glossary
Explanation of terms

ADJECTIVE - a word that describes a noun e.g. **'innocent'** (flower)

ALLITERATION - repetition of the same letter in words next to or near each other e.g. **'trumpet-tongued'**

ANAGNORISIS - moment when a character makes a crucial discovery e.g. Macbeth realises that the witches have tricked him

BLANK VERSE - verse without rhyme (poetry), especially verse using iambic pentameter

COMIC RELIEF - humorous scene that eases the tension e.g. the Porter's scene in Act 2

CONTRAST/JUXTAPOSITION - use of opposites e.g. **'flower'** and **'serpent'** are used to contrast with each other to show how wonderful the Macbeths look on the outside but how they are poisonous on the inside

DIALOGUE - conversation between characters

DRAMATIC IRONY - when the audience knows something the characters do not e.g. only the audience understands how ill-advised Duncan is to be addressing Macbeth as **'worthiest cousin'**

EPITHET - a descriptive phrase for a person e.g. **'brave Macbeth'**

ENJAMBMENT - when a sentence runs onto the next line

EXPOSITION - the beginning of a play or story

FOIL - something or someone that works as a contrast e.g. Macduff's emotion contrasts with Macbeth's lack of emotion

FORESHADOWING - to give a warning of a future event e.g. **'it will make us mad'**

FRAGMENTED SPEECH - speaking in short, incomplete sentences e.g. **'Out, I say!- one:two'**

HAMARTIA - a convention from Greek tragedy where the noble hero has a fatal weakness

HEPTAMETER - seven syllables/beats to a line

IAMBIC PENTAMETER - 10 syllables/beats to a line

IMAGE - powerful words or phrase that paints a picture in our heads e.g. the line **'all the perfumes of Arabia will not sweeten this little hand'** uses imagery to describe how guilty Lady Macbeth is feeling

IMPERATIVE VERBS - verbs that give orders e.g. **'Come, you spirits'**

INTERROGATIVE SENTENCE - a sentence that asks a question **'Are you a man?'**

JUXTAPOSITION - see contrast

MAJESTIC PLURAL PRONOUN - plural pronoun used by an individual of high rank e.g. Malcolm says **'We will perform'**

METAPHOR - descibing a person or object as something else e.g. **'My mind is full of scorpions'**

MODAL VERBS - verbs that show a level of certainty e.g. **'It will make us mad'**

MOTIF - a recurring idea in a book or play e.g. the idea of the lack of sleep

MONOSYLLABIC WORDS - words with one syllable - e.g. **'All this is so'**

NOUN - name of an object/place/time/emotion e.g. **'Macbeth/ butcher'**

PATHETIC FALLACY - when weather reflects the mood e.g. **'thunder and lightning'** in the opening scene

PARADOX - a contradictory sentence e.g. **'Fair is foul and foul is fair'**

PATHOS - sadness

PATRIARCHAL - a society where men are dominant/have power

PLOSIVE - hard sound made by a consonant 'd' 'b' 't' 'p' 'k' e.g. **'poor player'**

PLOT DEVICE - technique used to move narrative along

POSSESSIVE PRONOUN - word that shows something belongs to someone e.g. **'my dearest partner'**

PROSE - spoken language in ordinary form (not poetry) e.g. the Porter speaks in prose

RHYMING COUPLETS - pair of lines that both end in the same rhyming sound e.g. **'That calls upon us, by the grace of Grace/We will perform in measure, time and place.'**

REPETITION - when a word or phrase is repeated e.g. **'come, you spirits...come'**

RESOLUTION - the conclusion of a play when conflict is resolved

SETTING - where a scene is played out e.g. the opening setting is in a **'desolate place'**

SIMILE - describing a person or object as something else using 'like' or 'as' e.g. **'bear-like'**

SOLILOQUY - a speech where the character speaks his/her thoughts aloud.

SOUND EFFECT - a stage direction that adds to the aural effect e.g. **'an owl shrieks'**

STRUCTURE - the order in which a line/scene/play is put together

SUPERLATIVE - an adjective that describes something as the most or least e.g. **'dearest'**

SYMBOL - when an object/person stands for something else e.g **'babes'** are a symbol of innocence

SYNTAX - order of words in a sentence

TONE - mood or atmosphere

VERB - an action word e.g Lady Macbeth uses violent verbs such as **'pluck'd....dash'd'**